Discerning Vocations to Marriage, Celibacy and Singlehood

Discerning Vocations to Marriage, Celibacy and Singlehood

Marie Theresa Coombs, Hermit

and

Francis Kelly Nemeck, O.M.I.

Wipf and Stock Publishers

EUGENE, OREGON

Wipf and Stock Publishers
199 West 8th Avenue, Suite 3
Eugene, Oregon 97401

Discerning Vocations to Marriage, Celibacy and Singlehood
By Nemeck, Francis Kelly and Coombs, Marie Theresa

ISBN: 1-57910-784-2
Publication Date: October, 2001
Previously published by The Liturgical Press, 1994.

To
Christ Jesus,
The Light of the World

in
Heartfelt Appreciation
of
Kathleen Coombs

Lord, that I may see (Mark 10:51).

Contents

Principal Abbreviations

Called by God Francis Kelly Nemeck and Marie Theresa Coombs, *Called by God: A Theology of Vocation and Lifelong Commitment*, The Liturgical Press, 1991 (write The Liturgical Press, St. John's Abbey, Box 7500, Collegeville, MN 56321-7500; phone 1-800-858-5450; fax 1-800-445-5899).

CCSL *Corpus Christianorum Series Latina,* Brepols.

Contemplation Francis Kelly Nemeck and Marie Theresa Coombs, *Contemplation,* Michael Glazier, 1982, The Liturgical Press, 1990.

O Blessed Night Francis Kelly Nemeck and Marie Theresa Coombs, *O Blessed Night: Recovering from Addiction, Codependency and Attachment based on the Insights of St. John of the Cross and Pierre Teilhard de Chardin,* Alba House, 1991 (write: 2187 Victory Blvd., Staten Island, NY 10314; phone: 1-800-343-2522; fax 718-761-0057).

PL J. P. Migne, ed., *Patrologia Latina,* Brepols.

Receptivity Francis Kelly Nemeck, *Receptivity,* Vantage Press, 1985 (out of print).

Spiritual Direction Francis Kelly Nemeck and Marie Theresa Coombs, *The Way of Spiritual Direction,* Michael Glazier, 1985, The Liturgical Press, 1990.

Spiritual Journey Francis Kelly Nemeck and Marie Theresa Coombs, *The Spiritual Journey: Critical Thresholds and Stages of Adult Spiritual Genesis,* Michael Glazier, 1987, The Liturgical Press, 1990.

TDNT Gerhard Kittel and Gerhard Friedrich, eds., *Theological Dictionary of the New Testament*, I–X, Eerdmans, 1964–1977.

Introduction

Ask different people what the term "vocation" means, and you get a variety of responses. Many will say: "Vocation? For me, it suggests priesthood or religious life." Some may answer: "I see it as following God's will." Others might reply: "It's something we pray for an increase of at Mass on Sundays."

Seldom do we advert to the fact that vocation is a complex reality which affects the nitty-gritty of our lives for the duration of our earthly sojourn. In effect, most of us have at least three callings. Or to put it more precisely, our vocation comprises three intricately related aspects:

- *who* the Lord calls us *to be* (or, as it is often referred to, our self-identity),
- *how* the Lord calls us *to become* our unique selves in God (in other words, our vocational lifestyle),
- *what* the Lord calls us *to do* for God and for others (that is, our mission or ministry).

Who. We are called to be fully ourselves in God. Ultimately, that means a vocation to be whole persons deified in Father, Son and Spirit; a calling to be completely realized individuals transformed in God by participation.[1] In this life, we never know exactly who we are. Our deepest self remains beyond our grasp. Yet, as our faith intensifies, we receive increasing insight into this "who" of ours by means of a certain "comprehensive wisdom and spiritual understanding" (Col 1:9). That vague though impelling awareness flows primarily from

[1]See *Contemplation,* 16–18; *Spiritual Journey,* 19–21, 42–52.

a gradual, loving and intuitive experience of ourselves rather than from analytical, deductive and scientific reasoning.

How. There are many "hows" on our spiritual journey: the various aspects of discipleship (John 8:31; 13:35), the exercise of the corporal works of mercy (Matt 25:34-40), the implementation of the gifts of the Spirit (Gal 5:22), etc. Each of these contributes to the Lord's deification of us. Yet there is a special "how" which serves as an all-embracing milieu for the others: our vocational lifestyle. God calls us to personal divinization in the context of a certain way of life. Some vocational lifestyles are mutually exclusive, for example: married, single, celibate. Others coexist. For instance, the apostolic life can coexist with any of the above.

What. God brings everyone into this life to do something, to accomplish some mission, to make a positive contribution to the Body of Christ (Eph 4:12). Even a stillborn child can have a lifelong impact on the parents. Many people engage simultaneously in several missions, for example: administrator-educator-parent, doctor-teacher-director. Other people move through a succession of ministries or careers, for instance: nurse, chaplain, counselor. The possible combinations of apostolates to which God commissions us are myriad.

Vocationally speaking, who we are, how we are becoming and what we are sent to do initiate with God and redound to God. The fact that any one of us exists at all is not merely accidental. That our lifestyle is such and such is not purely arbitrary. That we are involved in a certain mission is not simply by chance. The Lord chooses us to be unique persons, to become ourselves in a certain manner and to bear fruit, fruit that will last (John 15:16).

The more we mature, the more the various aspects of our vocation interconnect. Ordinarily, we cannot be our true self in the Lord until we become that self in the way that God wills and until we do what God desires. In a sense, our lifestyle is the matrix of our evolving self-identity, while our ministry is an especially providential means to the fullness of the other two.

We can compare the interrelatedness of the three aspects of the mystery we name "vocation" to the interaction of our right brain, left brain and central nervous system; or again to the interdependence of our lungs, heart and circulatory system. Each organ functions as an essential part of an extremely complex whole. Yet, we can single out one organ for careful examination.

Regarding the three interrelated aspects of calling, our prime focus in this book is Christian lifestyle—our vocational "how." That aspect of vocation refers to the God-given and all-embracing context in which we live and mature in every respect: emotional, intellectual, social, affective, spiritual, etc.

Christians the world over are in search of a vibrant sense of vocation. They seek in faith to understand what it means to be called personally by God. In an earlier book of ours entitled *Called by God,* we offered a theology of vocation and lifelong commitment from an evolutionary and relational perspective. First, we presented this mystery in the light of God's will and our destiny. Second, we synthesized the rich biblical data found in such notions as choosing, calling and consecrating. Third, we elaborated a theology of burgeoning vocation and progressive consciousness up to a vocational awareness mature enough to sustain permanent commitment. In describing that process we compared our insights with those of several renowned authors in the field of developmental psychology. Fourth, we described the general pattern characteristic of vocational evolution, developing consciousness and deepening commitment in the later stages of the spiritual journey.

As important as that theology of vocation is, another crucial issue remains—its practical application to Christian lifestyles. What principles guide us in the discernment of the Lord's will as it pertains to our calling? How do we arrive at a better understanding of *who* we are called to be, of *how* we are called to become ourselves and of *what* we are called to do for God and for others? How do we discern which vocational choices to make?

Besides having a general awareness of being called by God, Christians need to be able to discern their particular vocation. In this book we take up the practical question of discernment with respect to what can be termed basic vocational lifestyles. These are specifically three: marriage, celibacy and singlehood.

Our principal objective in this book is to identify and to explain principles of discernment which indicate the authenticity of a possible vocation to marriage, celibacy or singlehood. We are concerned principally with that peak experience in our evolving vocational consciousness during which we undergo our calling in terms of an existential inability to become otherwise.[2]

That threshold frequently occurs in the course of what we have termed in a previous work "Immersion in Creation for Christ."[3] Regarding Christian development, that vocational peak experience ushers us into mature discipleship. Jesus invites us to follow him ever more knowingly, voluntarily and perseveringly. Mature discipleship implies consciously pursuing a more authentic self-identity. Seasoned discipleship postulates living intensely the lifestyle which the Lord has given us. Adult discipleship necessitates faithfully accomplishing the mission entrusted to us.

In view of more authentic discipleship, the underlying purpose of this book is to discern *how* to follow Jesus more genuinely. Having been called by God, I am thereby the Lord's disciple. What then is the providential milieu, the graced environment, the gifted context in which my self-identity develops and out of which my mission unfolds? It is my vocational lifestyle.

As we probe marriage, celibacy and singlehood, we describe these vocational lifestyles as if we were viewing three peaks. Most of us pilgrims continue to struggle somewhere along the slopes or in the valleys. Yet, we are advancing toward the heights. We accentuate the peaks not to overwhelm but to challenge. We stress not so much where we are but where we are heading, with God's grace. We emphasize the ideal because to such has God called us:

> Be perfect
> as your heavenly Father is perfect (Matt 5:48).
>
> Love . . .
> as I have loved you (John 15:12).

[2]We adapt this expression from a similar one used by Edward Schillebeeckx in *Celibacy* (New York: Sheed & Ward, 1968) 21–25, 120–129. See *Called by God,* 92, 99–132 (esp. 108–110).

[3]See *Spiritual Journey,* 55–74 (esp. 60–61).

Before focusing on the peaks, however, let us review certain fundamental notions related to discernment in general and vocational discernment in particular.

* * *

1) All translations from Hebrew, Greek, Latin, French and Spanish sources—including biblical—are our own. Ordinarily, we adapt those texts to reflect contemporary inclusive language.

2) We deeply respect the need for inclusive language in theological discourse. Yet, contemporary English poses many problems in this regard. To strike a balance between those two factors, we follow these guidelines:

a) When employing singular pronouns to refer to the human person, we always use s/he, him/her.

b) Although many people consider the nouns "God" and "Lord" as masculine in gender, we readily acknowledge the feminine dimension of God and the legitimacy of speaking of God as "Mother." To avoid using a masculine pronoun in reference to God and Lord, we ordinarily repeat the noun.

c) Regarding "Father," especially in biblical texts, we sometimes use the masculine pronoun when repetition of the noun would be cumbersome.

d) Regarding Jesus, we employ the masculine pronoun in reference to him. We do the same with respect to the titles "Christ," "Son" and "Lord."

e) Regarding the Holy Spirit, we usually avoid any pronoun and repeat the noun.

FUNDAMENTAL NOTIONS

CHAPTER 1

Christian Vocational Lifestyles

As the biblical authors put it: Willing us to exist, God knows us and chooses us to be. Having chosen us, the Lord calls us each by name and consecrates us.[1] That choosing, calling and consecrating we term "our vocation."

Our vocation is both eternal and temporal. It is eternal because even before forming us in the womb the Lord had already consecrated us (Jer 1:5). Moreover, our eternity will consist in the everlasting realization of that consecration—unending, ever-deepening communion with Father, Son and Spirit. Our vocation is also temporal because it unfolds in space and time. It extends from the moment of inception to the instant of death.[2] Thus, we experience a vocation within a vocation—a temporal particular calling to a self-identity, a lifestyle and a mission within an eternal universal call to holiness.

In several respects, our eternal vocation corresponds to *who* the Lord is calling us to be. Who we are destined to be are unique persons transformed in God by God. Who we have been foreknown, chosen and called to be are singular individuals deified and divinized by participation in the life of the Trinity. This self-identity and transformation begin with inception and develop slowly throughout our earthly sojourn.[3]

Our temporal vocation, on the other hand, corresponds primarily to *how* that spiritual journey unfolds in the here and

[1]See *Called by God,* 39–69.

[2]See *Spiritual Journey,* 19–21, 42–45.

[3]See ibid., 39–52.

now as well as to *what* we do for God and for others. How we become is distinguishable from what we are commissioned to do. "How" refers to vocational lifestyle. "What" refers to ministry, apostolate or mission in this life. Discerning the basic Christian lifestyles of marriage, celibacy and singlehood is the subject of this book.

A. The Phrase "Vocational Lifestyle"

In contemporary English, "lifestyle" refers to an individual's typical way of living. People speak of "the lifestyles of the rich and famous," "hippie lifestyle," "middle-class lifestyle," etc. Because of these common and at times pejorative associations, some persons object to using the term in relation to Christian vocation. Others deem that "style" is too weak a noun to express the mystery of calling. We admit validity in both objections. As a matter of fact, we frequently use other turns of speech in our writings to describe this aspect of calling: "way of life," "mode of living," "manner of becoming." Nonetheless, while recognizing its limitations, we retain a certain partiality for the word "lifestyle."

In reference to vocation, our understanding of the term "lifestyle" is specific and restricted:

> *Life* bespeaks that life which God has given us and the fullness of life to which the Lord has destined us. This life is from God, to God and sustained by God.
>
> *Style* indicates mode, manner, way of actualizing that life. It is both the dominating vocational milieu or matrix in which that life unfolds and the key providential catalyst which thrusts that life toward maturity.
>
> *Lifestyle* then is a compound word which indicates the junction where our *zoé* (the life by which we live; God's life in us—John 10:10, 14:6) merges with our *bíos* (the life which we live; our mortal process—1 Tim 2:2).[4]

There are many lifestyles which can legitimately be called Christian. In this book we accentuate three such vocations:

[4]See *TDNT,* II:832-872.

marriage, celibacy and singlehood.[5] Each one constitutes a relatively self-contained calling.

By ''self-contained'' we mean that the basic elements of a particular mode of living are sufficient for holistic personal growth. An authentic celibate, for instance, attains fulfillment primarily through solitude, community and some ministry. S/he does not need a spouse and children to experience wholeness of being. However, we qualify ''self-contained'' with ''relatively'' because not one of these three vocational lifestyles exists alone. Each of them compenetrates and coexists with at least one other. Most married, celibate and single persons, for instance, are called also to some form of the apostolic life.

A vocational lifestyle in the strict sense entails more than a vague thrust toward a certain way of Christian living. For example, an authentic calling to marriage cannot be complete until the person experiences a vocation to marry someone in particular. Two people receive not only a general calling to the conjugal life, but also a specific vocation to marry each other.

A vocational lifestyle involves a fundamental way of becoming our true selves and of relating to others. It is an all-embracing, all-penetrating mode of living, of thinking about ourselves and of interacting with others.

Our vocational ''how'' is all-embracing, because every facet of our daily existence falls within the parameters of its influence. It extends meaning and relevance to every aspect of our life. How God calls us to live, as well as how we respond to that vocation, directly affects our ups and downs, our likes and dislikes, our hopes and fears, our present and future.

Our vocational lifestyle is all-penetrating too. If I am married, for instance, the reality of the conjugal ''we-us'' permeates all the details of my life. The covenant between my spouse and myself impacts every pain and joy, every hesitation and decision of my concrete existence.

Our vocational ''how'' contributes immeasurably to our

[5]Other vocational lifestyles could be mentioned, for example: the religious life, the monastic life, the apostolic life, the contemplative life, the eremitical life. And there are still others: different forms of communes, like an Israeli kibbutz; various kinds of ashrams, whether Christian or Hindu; etc.

self-identity and self-awareness. God has destined us to a transformation which we cannot begin to imagine (1 Cor 2:9). The depth of our inner poverty is so far beyond our comprehension that it leaves us reeling (Rom 7:21). Yet, through our lifestyle we receive increasing insight into who we are and how we are to become our true self in God.

Our vocational lifestyle determines to a large degree our rapport with others. If I am single, for instance, I may date several people. However, if I am married or celibate and wish to remain faithful to my calling, I will not be available for dating—even though I take a close friend out for lunch, a stroll through the park or a drive along the beach.

Because of who we are and how we are becoming, we make certain choices. If we were different, we would have to opt another way. Our mode of living is to a large degree an extension of ourselves. Who we are precedes how we live and what we do. Yet, our God-willed lifestyle also radically influences our personhood.

Ask a woman, for example: "Who are you?" She may reply: "Ms. Jane Brown Smith." That is: "I am Jane Brown, wife of John Smith." Her marital vocation directly qualifies who she is. Similarly, Jane's husband, by virtue of their marriage, is no longer simply an "I." He has become, by reason of their mutual vocational lifestyle, a "we" (Matt 19:6). His wife is not his in a possessive sense, but to him and with him. She is a unique gift of God in his life and an equal partner in a covenant. His interior and exterior being is specified by Jane and the relationship they share. He chooses his employment and ministry in accord with their shared vocational lifestyle. What he does or does not do with his leisure flows out of how he and she are becoming. His married life modifies his rapport with all other women, including his mother (Gen 2:24; Matt 19:5). His physical dwelling, his living habits, the car he drives, the company he keeps—all possess a relatedness to her. Marriage radically changes his decision-making process. Who is he? He is John Smith, husband of Jane Brown.

The Gospel According to Mark presents an interesting insight into the disciples' evolving consciousness of the self-identity of Jesus, his way of life and his mission. Mark accentuates two decisive questions in the course of his sixteen-chapter narrative. First, on the lips of a myriad of people he puts the question, either expressed or implied: "Who is this man?" Peter eventually proclaims: "You are the Christ" (Mark 8:29). Then, from that threshold at Caesarea Philippi the pivotal issue becomes: "Who is the Christ?" Jesus proceeds to reveal the authentic Messiah. This revelation reaches its climax on Calvary when the Roman centurian confesses his divinity: "Truly, this man was the Son of God" (Mark 15:39). Thus, the revelation in Mark of who Jesus is progresses from "this man" to "the Christ" to "the Son of God."

Who, then, is Jesus? He is the Christ, truly God and truly human. How, therefore, is Jesus? His Christ-identity developed in the context of his becoming fully human in such a way that his divinity gradually permeated and ultimately transformed his humanity. The apex of that process was his death-resurrection. Jesus's lifestyle was that of the theandric Christ, unique in all salvation history.

The mysterious reality of the Christ-event does not fit into conventional categories. Nonetheless, most people would say that Jesus was celibate. Certainly, he was not married, and he was other than single. Surely his mission was beyond anything that we can conceptualize. The vocational "who," "how" and "what" of Jesus dovetail into one: the "Word made flesh" (John 1:14); "the Christ, the Son of the living God" (Matt 16:16); "the Lord" (1 Cor 12:3). Our vocational lifestyles and missions, however, are distinguishable, even though they remain profoundly integrated with our personal development.

Our vocational lifestyle, then, is a dynamic gift from God. It is to us, yet not of us. It is for us, but not a possession to do with as we please. Our lifestyle specifies our way of becoming both within ourselves and in relation to others. It radically influences our self-perception as well as our rapport with our evolving self, with other persons and with the diverse situations around us. It must be nurtured, challenged and let go when the time is ripe to move on. Our lifestyle is always ongoing, constantly developing, increasingly Christogenic.[6]

Thus, as far as our vocational "how" is concerned, we never have it made. Our Christian lifestyle unfolds to us as well as with us.

[6]As in "Christogenesis." See *Receptivity,* 10–11; *Spiritual Journey,* 19–20.

B. Three "Basic" Vocational Lifestyles

We speak of the vocational lifestyles of marriage, celibacy and singlehood as "basic" in three senses:

> 1) These distinct callings serve as foundations to other ways of living and acting. Not only do these modes of becoming coexist with other vocational lifestyles, but also in relation to them they act as does a base to the rest of an edifice.
>
> 2) Ordinarily, each of these three remains exclusive of the other two. Usually, we do not find the same individual simultaneously married and single, married and celibate or single and celibate.
>
> 3) These basic modes of living are all-inclusive in the sense that each spiritually adult Christian is either married, celibate or single.

The vocational lifestyles of marriage and celibacy are analogous to the outermost rays of a spectrum. Singlehood would then be like the middle. We all start off single. Most marry. Many remain single. A few become celibate. Just as multiple shades of color exist within the spectrum and blend imperceptibly one into the other, so too there are variations within and overlappings among these lifestyles.

While God does not ordinarily call a person to two basic vocational lifestyles at the same time, we discover in the history of spirituality certain unique situations:

> 1) We find instances of "virginal marriages." Catholic tradition believes that such was the case between Mary and Joseph. The supposition is that their marriage and others like theirs are not consummated because of Christ and the Gospel. We would, however, term the lifestyle of these persons "married" rather than "celibate" because they continue living together in an all-embracing and all-penetrating spousal, though non-genital, relationship.
>
> 2) Examples of nonconsummated marriages exist in which sexual intercourse does not occur for reasons of illness, impotency or a choice other than Christ and the

Gospel. People in such marriages may or may not engage in erotic love expressions, and may or may not live in covenanted intimacy.

3) There are also a few instances of marriages in which sexual intercourse occurs for a while, but at a certain point both spouses agree out of a sense of calling to cease all genital expression of their love. In some of these cases, the cessation is only temporary. In other marriages, it endures for the rest of the couple's wedded life. However long it lasts, the man and woman remain married, but engage in a sort of eschatological living out of their marriage. For this direction to be an authentic vocation, both spouses must simultaneously experience the same calling.

When the genital expression of love has not existed at all or at some point ceases in a marriage as a result of an authentic vocation, some people refer to this living together as "celibate marriage." In reality, however, the couple's basic lifestyle remains more married than celibate. There is much more to married life—as an all-embracing and all-penetrating mode of interacting—than sexual intercourse. Conversely, celibacy consists of much more than abstinence from erotic expression of love.

The cessation of genital intimacy occurs in some marriages due to factors such as boredom, alienation or irreconcilable differences. Some couples in this situation continue to live under the same roof, while going their separate ways. In effect, this option smacks more of single rather than married life.

When medical considerations cause husbands and wives to terminate the genital expression of their love, many of these couples remain far more married than either celibate or single in their basic lifestyle. In these cases, interpersonal intimacy and conjugal covenant are not affected adversely by the medical factor.

Reflecting for a moment on the few considerations above, the reader begins to appreciate how complicated any discussion of specific vocational lifestyles becomes. It is often very difficult to discern in the concrete where one lifestyle leaves off and another begins. Yet, this ambiguity need not stop us from trying to understand more deeply the faith dimension underlying vocational discernment and commitment.

We speak, therefore, of marriage, celibacy and singlehood not as clear-cut categories or parallel lines. Rather, we see them as accents in a certain ebb and flow of innumerable and inscrutable forms of actualization.

C. Similarities and Differences among These Lifestyles

Marriage, celibacy and singlehood as Christian vocations have this in common: Each postulates its own spiritual imperative.[7] Spouses, celibates, single persons experience from within themselves the following truth: "I can best become myself transformed in God by freely embracing my particular calling."

As a Christian vocation, marriage is a formally vowed lifestyle. Persons living the celibate life also ordinarily take vows, although not necessarily in a publicly professed fashion. The single life is not usually vowed. However, all three lifestyles—as Christian modes of becoming—are equally committed ways of living. They are authentic callings on equal footing before God. None is better in itself than another. One is "better" only for the person whom God so calls.

In marriage, each spouse vows in love to the other the sharing of this earthly existence. In celibacy, the person vows, promises or dedicates in love his/her mortal life to Christ. In singlehood, persons live the single life for some time, and at a certain point some choose positively to remain single.

God transforms two spouses both directly one-to-one and indirectly through each other and through their marital covenant. The Lord transforms a celibate both directly one-to-one and indirectly through relationships and the celibate life itself. God transforms a single person both directly one-to-one and indirectly through relationships and the single life itself.

The various ministries to which God sends married, celibate and single persons are also effective instruments for their personal divinization. Vocational lifestyles and ministerial pursuits interrelate to form a multifaceted but integrated vocation.

[7]See *Called by God,* 122, 127–132.

All three basic vocational lifestyles entail a consecration on the Lord's part, because through each of them God makes the person holy. Marriage and celibacy also necessarily evoke from those so called a personal consecration. Spouses consecrate themselves to each other and together they consecrate their marriage to God. A celibate, by definition, has consecrated him/herself and his/her life directly to God. Single persons, by vocation, are not usually consecrated to God in either of the above two ways, although they remain consecrated by God.

When people pray "for vocations," most think spontaneously of "the priesthood" and "the religious life." The presbyteral office, strictly speaking, is a ministry—a vocational *what* to which God calls a few. Moreover, there can exist within that calling a variety of further vocational refinements: missionary, pastor, prison chaplain, etc. A priest may or may not be a personally consecrated celibate. Interiorly, some priests are in reality more "single" than celibate. Experience proves also that a few priests are in fact more "married" than single. The religious life, on the other hand, is properly speaking a vocational *how,* with consecrated celibacy at its core. As a specific lifestyle, the religious life consists of a celibate calling combined with a vocation to some other lifestyle, for example: the apostolic or the contemplative life, the monastic or the eremitical life.

CHAPTER 2

Vocational Discernment

In the childhood and the adolescent stages of our spiritual journey, we tend to be concerned primarily with living according to the customs, practices and norms which other persons designate as appropriate for good Christians. Initially, our spiritual life centers around external events, rites and behaviors. In these early stages we perceive God as somewhat distant; we honor and respect Christ, but we do not ordinarily have a sense of mature intimacy with him.

However, at some point along the way, we experience Jesus as friend. We see him as someone with whom we yearn to share deeply. We realize that he loves us personally; that he cares for us individually; that he influences our lives directly.

That experience of an interpersonal relationship with the risen Lord marks a radical threshold in our spiritual development.[1] We are henceforth Christian adults and desire that every facet of our personal life develop in reference to Jesus. We want also to let go whatever impedes us from deepening this newfound friendship with Christ.

Thus, we begin reexamining where we are heading. We reevaluate our spiritual direction. That reassessment of the meaning and purpose of life inevitably raises the question of vocation and its discernment.

A. Discerning

In common English the verb *to discern* means to come to know, recognize or identify one thing as distinct from some-

[1]See *Spiritual Journey,* 55–61.

thing else; to see or understand the difference between several issues or options. The noun *discernment,* therefore, designates the ability to grasp skillfully and to comprehend accurately the truth which lies beyond mere appearances. Discernment is closely associated with:

- *discrimination,* which emphasizes a capacity for distinguishing and selecting the excellent or the appropriate;
- *perception,* which implies intuitive cognition and heightened sensitivity in evaluating situations;
- *penetration,* which suggests a searching mind that goes beyond the obvious or the superficial;
- *insight,* which accentuates depth of resourcefulness coupled with empathy;
- *acumen,* which denotes consistent astuteness accompanied by shrewd soundness of judgment.

1) *Discernment in the New Testament*

In the primitive Christian community, we find a number of words which express something of what is understood today as discernment.[2] Several of these terms are variations of the verb *kríno* whose basic meaning is to separate, to distinguish, to estimate, to judge. Two variations come closest to discernment in the theological sense: *ana-kríno* (to judge between, to examine closely, to distinguish among) and *dia-kríno* (to sift through, to pierce beyond, to go to the heart of). The prefix *aná* is frequently translated by "between" and *diá* by "through."

In a dispute with the Pharisees and the Sadducees, Matthew places *dia-kríno* on the lips of Jesus:

> You know how to discern the face of the heavens.
> Why can you not interpret the signs of the times? (Matt 16:3).

Discerning in that text implies the ability to perceive what is taking place from God's perspective. It is the capacity to understand what the Lord is revealing through current events. Jesus laments that although the signs are present the capability to receive and to interpret them is not.

[2]See *TDNT,* I:187–188; II:225–260; III:921–954.

The author of the Letter to the Hebrews uses the noun form of *dia-kríno* to describe an essential quality of mature Christians:

> They are persons trained by practice
> for the discernment of good and evil (Heb 5:14).

Here, discernment is related to self-discipline tested over a period of time. It is directed toward moral issues and behavioral attitudes. In the context, the author chides the community because it has not yet attained that maturity—the adulthood of "solid food"—but is "still subsisting on baby milk" (Heb 5:13-14).

In his First Letter to the Corinthians, Paul employs *ana-kríno* and *dia-kríno* several times, both in noun form and in verb form. We highlight three passages.

First, in the context of the dispute in the Church at Corinth over true and false wisdom, the Apostle to the Gentiles uses *ana-kríno* twice:

> An unspiritual person is not receptive
> to the things of God's Spirit,
> for they are foolishness to him/her
> Moreover, an unspiritual person cannot know them
> because spiritual things can only be discerned spiritually.
> The spiritual person, on the other hand,
> discerns everything (1 Cor 2:14-15).

In that passage the author links directly our ability to discern with the indwelling and spiritualizing activity of the Holy Spirit. This discernment, however, not only pertains to the spiritual realm, but also extends to every facet of life. For the spiritual person can recognize the presence of God in all things.

Second, in the context of decorum for public worship in general and for the Lord's Supper in particular, Paul employs *dia-kríno* in his warning:

> A person ought to examine him/herself
> before eating this bread and drinking this cup.
> Whoever eats and drinks without discerning
> the Body [and the Blood of the Lord]
> eats and drinks his/her own judgment (1 Cor 11:28-29).

In that admonition, the author focuses specifically on the

faith dimension of discernment. One can distinguish ordinary bread and wine from the Eucharist only by faith.

Third, in the context of the charisms, Paul mentions the noun *diákrisis* as a spiritual gift:

> To one there is given . . . prophecy,
> and to another the discernings of spirits . . . (1 Cor 12:8, 10).

Both nouns related to discernment in the above text are plural: discernings and spirits. There are ''discernings'' in the sense of many issues to be addressed: discerning a spiritual gift of an individual, discerning a charism of an entire community, etc. The focus of the discernings is also myriad: ''spirits.'' A variety of spirits exists, and the distinctions among them are not always immediately apparent. Both the transforming activity of the indwelling Trinity and the destructive tendency of egocentrism (Rom 7:14-25) operate within us. For that reason, another New Testament author advises:

> Do not believe every spirit.
> Rather test the spirits
> to see whether they are from God (1 John 4:1).

Thus, discernment is a special gift which enables the recipient to sift through the maze of conflicting influences.

In the First Letter to the Corinthians, Paul presents ''discernments of spirits'' as a charism given only to certain persons (1 Cor 12:4-11). Yet, earlier in the same letter, he infers that any adult Christian can discern ''everything'' (1 Cor 2:10-16), and again that all believers should be able to distinguish between table bread and the Body of the Lord (1 Cor 11:28-29). Is the ability to discern then bestowed on everyone or on a few? The gift whereby one person enters directly into discernment with another—for instance, in a spiritual director-directee relationship—is a charism given only to some.[3] On the other hand, integral to maturing as a Christian is the increasing ability to discern God's will in one's life. Capability for vocational discernment is a gift which the Lord furnishes to every adult believer.[4]

[3]See *Spiritual Direction,* 33–50, 83–94.

[4]See *Spiritual Journey,* 60–61.

2) *Discernment in General*

Ordinarily, discernment denotes a process for ascertaining by faith something of God's will in a given instance. Or again, it is a process directed toward experiencing in faith a basic synchronicity with the Lord in regard to a specific issue.

That faith process is influenced by numerous interacting factors: for example, the Word of God in Scripture, the living tradition of the Church, the confluence of Divine Providence, a person's intuition and common sense. As a *faith* process, discernment remains obscure and always contains an element of risk. Yet, even though faith is beyond reason and feeling, it is not thereby necessarily without some reason and feeling.

The steps in a discernment process are essentially four: 1) gathering pertinent information and identifying possible options; 2) searching out and testing the options which seem most viable; 3) deciding upon a course of action and taking a stand; 4) seeking confirmation regarding what is of God in the decision. Since most discernment is ongoing, the discernee continues after the decision to be receptive to any corrections or modifications which the Spirit may introduce.

Discernment is something in which we take an active role. We seek; we search; we decide; we confirm. Yet, it is also something that we receive. God gives us the ability to seek, to search, to decide and to confirm. Moreover, it is the Spirit who generates harmony, peace and joy within the discernee.

Discernment is holistic because it involves the whole person and redounds to the qualitative progress of the whole person. Discernment is spiritual because it is from the Spirit and differentiates between the spirits within us and around us.

B. Discerning Vocation

Ultimately, our vocation consists in God calling us to consummate loving union with Father, Son and Spirit for all eternity. During the course of our earthly sojourn our vocation comprises three aspects: a self-identity, or who the Lord calls us to be; a lifestyle, or how the Lord calls us to become ourselves in God; a mission, or what the Lord calls us to do for God and others.

Many of us receive the basic thrust of this threefold vocation at inception. This calling is an impulse, a movement, a direction which remains integral to God's gift to us of our personhood.[5] As we evolve throughout our spiritual journey, so too does each aspect of our vocation. Our initial personal encounter with Jesus—as well as each subsequent threshold of interior genesis—gives rise to an urgent need for a renewed understanding of the meaning and content of our calling.[6]

The faith process whereby we listen to God, sift out our various interior leanings and try to name the Lord's particular invitation to us we term "vocational discernment."[7] We cannot do the Father's will until we first listen to him, and we cannot know what the Father desires of us until he furnishes us some insight into his design. In vocational discernment, therefore, we seek enlightenment from God with regard to our self-identity, lifestyle and mission. We search for insight into the manner in which we can more faithfully respond to the Lord's calling and more voluntarily cooperate with God's initiative.

All three aspects of vocation require ongoing discernment. In this book, however, we focus on the discernment of callings to three Christian lifestyles: marriage, celibacy and singlehood.

C. The Significance of Vocational Discernment

The core of Christian life is love. Jesus invites all his disciples:

> Love the Lord your God
> with your whole heart . . . soul . . . mind and . . .
> strength. . .
> Love your neighbor as yourself (Mark 12:29-31).

Elsewhere, Jesus calls us to love our neighbor not only as ourselves, but specifically as the Father loves him (John 15:9) and as he himself loves us (John 15:12).

[5]See ibid., 39–52; *Called by God,* 29–35, 65–69.

[6]See *Called by God,* 143–150.

[7]See *Spiritual Direction,* 15–32, 51–118; *Called by God,* 68–69, 137–139.

Fidelity to a calling to marriage, celibacy or singlehood is a concrete way in which we actualize our love for God and creation. Discernment of our vocational lifestyle thus has significance 1) for our personal transformation in God and 2) for our prophetic mission within the Church and to the world.

1) *For Personal Transformation*

God's love is both diffusive and unitive. On the one hand, it radiates out from the Trinity, calling all creation into being and sustaining it in existence. On the other hand, the Lord's love unifies and transforms the entirety of creation. It converges creation toward optimum fulfillment, which is the reconciliation of all in Christ (Col 1:15-20).

As for humankind, God's diffusive and unitive love manifests itself in a specifically personal and intimate manner. The Son, together with the Father and the Spirit, offers himself to us in tender love, while at the same time inviting us to freely surrender ourselves and our world to him.

The union to which God calls us transforms us. We are to become deified: that is, to be divinized by participation in the Trinity's own inner life.[8] God creates and re-creates us in God's own likeness (Gen 1:27; Eph 4:24; Col 3:10). The Lord configures us to the image of Christ (Rom 8:29) who himself is the icon of the Father (Col 1:15). God accomplishes all this in and by the Spirit (1 Pet 1:2).

Our individual deification lies at the core of our vocation. The Lord chooses us, calls us to holiness and consecrates us so that we can become transformed in God in a uniquely personal way. A vocation to marriage, celibacy or singlehood constitutes a particularly significant context for that transforming process. Thus, vocational discernment and our response to it contribute directly to our divinization.

Since marriage, celibacy and singlehood form the basic God-given modes which express *how* we become our deified selves, each of these vocations has an intrinsic value all its own. Each vocational lifestyle exerts its own transforming and purifying effect. In this way, an authentic calling to marriage, celibacy

[8]See *Contemplation,* 16–20; *Spiritual Direction,* 15–32.

or singlehood also interacts with our vocational "who." It fosters the emergence of a maturing self-identity. Thus, our lifestyle constitutes a crucial matrix in which, through which and out of which our self-identity moves toward completion.

2) *For Prophetic Mission/Ministry*

Our basic lifestyle is furthermore intimately related to our vocational "what." A vocation to marriage, celibacy or singlehood greatly influences what God sends us forth to do. Our positive response to the Lord's calling to a certain lifestyle increases our capacity for prophetic mission and ministry within the Church and to the world.

Jesus himself spoke of the need for discernment in relation to the implementation of prophetic mission:

> When you see a cloud looming up in the west,
> you say at once that rain is coming. And so it does.
> When the wind is from the south,
> you say that it will be hot. And so it is.
> Hypocrites! You know how to interpret earth and sky.
> Why is it that you do not know how to discern this present time?
> (Luke 12:54-56).

What is "this present time"?—this *kairós;* this graced moment? Ultimately, it is the incarnation of God in human history and the recapitulation of all creation in Christ (Eph 1:10). It designates the reign of God already operative within us (Luke 17:21) and all around us (Mark 1:15).

"This present time" refers also to the nitty-gritty of each person's salvation history and to the concrete manner in which each one cooperates in the prophetic mission of Jesus. In this sense, the phrase can sustain a variety of meanings.

Most of us possess adequate skills for deciphering the more obvious aspects of life. Take the weather, for instance: A clear blue sky probably means that we can go ahead with our plans to spend the day at the beach. Heavy dark clouds, on the other hand, indicate that we had better gear toward some indoor activity. Food offers another example: We know that overeating causes excessive weight, while too little nourishment leads to fatigue. In the context of work, common sense tells us that we must balance our activity with some leisure. If not, we burn out. On the other hand, if we relax to the point of neglecting our responsibilities we end up dissipated.

Other areas of interpretation may be just as important, but the direction less obvious. Take for instance the political arena: Choosing between this candidate or that, this party or that—especially when each one has obvious strengths and weaknesses—can be frustrating. International diplomacy and world trade are other examples, along with justice and peace, global disarmament, world hunger, ecological concerns, etc.

Reading the signs of "this present time" is indeed perplexing. Yet, as Christians we have a moral obligation to inform ourselves about what is going on in our local, national and global communities. We must do our best to sift out truth from falsehood, to discern and to act upon the directions which lead to qualitative progress.

That responsibility pertains to the prophetic dimension of Christian commitment. We are called to be seers, to look around and to view the world as God sees it from within. We are commissioned to become involved in the world in a way that facilitates the Spirit's recapitulation of all in Christ (Eph 1:10). We are called to labor actively for peace, justice and sanctification.

Effective exercise of the prophetic dimension of Christian life requires that we come to terms with our individual vocations. To have a prophetic impact, we need to find the basic way in which God calls each of us to personally contribute to the development of this world for Christ. We have to be prophet within ourselves before we can be prophet to society. We have to prepare through vocational discernment and commitment the way for Christ's coming within us before we can prepare his way in the world.

CHAPTER 3

Limitations on Vocational Discernment

Jesus was plainly distressed by the crowd's inability to perceive the graced moment offered by God: "Hypocrites! . . . How is it that you do not know how to discern this present time?"—this *kairós* (Luke 12:56)? Perhaps the key to a response lies in a question which Christ on another occasion put to his disciples: "How is it that you still have so little faith?" (Mark 4:40).

Since discernment is a faith process, any lack of faith constitutes a formidable obstacle to discerning vocational lifestyle. Yet, the presence of faith—even deep faith—paradoxically imposes limits on our capacity to grasp God's will.

Five factors related to faith restrict our ability to discern vocational lifestyles. They are: a) the mystery itself of vocation, b) limitations inherent in the mediums of human interaction, c) misconceptions surrounding the very notion of vocation, d) insufficiencies in popular theologies of vocation, and e) lack of practical guidance for so many people seeking vocational discernment.

A. Limitations Deriving from Vocation as Mystery

We can never reduce our vocation to a clear-cut logical way of proceeding in life. At best, what we grasp of our calling at any given moment is its general flow. For instance, two persons may marry out of a sense of divine calling. Yet, the specific manner in which that marriage evolves, the particulars of the couple's response, the concrete milieu in which they live out their calling, unfold only on a day-to-day basis.

Even when we do identify certain aspects of our vocational direction, our insight remains largely superficial. We can never adequately comprehend the full depth and scope of God's activity within us and through us.

Each of us is a mystery. Not only is it impossible for another person to know us totally, but we can never in this life fully plumb our own depths. We cannot possess complete self-knowledge.

> Lord . . . you created my inmost being;
> you formed me in my mother's womb . . .
> A mystery am I,
> as are all your works (Ps 139:13-14).

God's calling is integral to our personhood. As we cannot fully comprehend ourselves, neither can we understand completely the Lord's design for us.

> How deep are the riches and the wisdom of God!
> How inscrutable the Lord's judgments!
> How unfathomable God's ways!
> Who has ever penetrated the mind of the Lord? (Rom 11:33-34).

B. Limitations Inherent in the Mediums of Human Interaction

The fact that God's calling is so personal to each individual also limits vocational discernment. If your calling to celibacy or my vocation to singlehood is so unique, what is the use of formulating general principles? If Christian marriage is such a mystery (Eph 5:32), how can anyone articulate specific principles which are commonly applicable? To respond to those questions, it is helpful to reflect on three interrelated mediums of human interchange: concepts, institutions and models.

1) *Concepts*

When we understand something, we tend to conceptualize what we know. When we think, we give names to the objects of our thoughts. Those concepts are derived from our experience of reality, and they in turn help us to relate more reflectively with the persons, the events and the relationships which constitute our evolving world.

Even though in this mortal existence our vocation remains a profound mystery, there arises a need to put our experience into a communicable framework. Theology is faith seeking understanding. The faith dimension of theology entails receptivity to the insight which divine revelation brings to bear on a given issue. The understanding dimension of theology implies the recognition of what observation, reasoning and intuition tell us about the matter at hand. As our faith and understanding come together, our intelligence tries to introduce some order into that quest. We attempt to conceptualize the fruit of our search. God, for instance, calls us, and we name that "vocation." The Lord calls us, furthermore, to a personalized way of becoming, and we name that "lifestyle."

In a sense, the formation of concepts limits and hence impoverishes the potential vastness of understanding. Yet, use of concepts helps to organize and to prioritize knowledge. Provided that we can let them go, concepts serve as meaningful points of departure for further insight and deeper understanding. They are instruments, not ends in themselves.

To introduce order, to name or to conceptualize does not imply needless categorizing, oversimplifying or casting in concrete. The latter activities do regretfully occur all too frequently. Rather than reflect authentic theologizing, some approaches to mystery represent frightful abuses of human intelligence and de facto denial of the transcendent immanence of God.[1]

When we try to describe the content of our concepts of marriage, celibacy and singlehood, we observe an interesting phenomenon. We find greater difficulty in attempting to formulate the essential elements of celibacy than those of marriage. Furthermore, we discover that the inherent qualities of singlehood are even more elusive than those of celibacy. Thus, in comparing those three basic lifestyles, we encounter a decreasing effectiveness in terms of human ability to conceptualize them.

[1]See *Called by God,* 11–12.

2) *Institutions*

Personal interaction frequently gives rise to some form of institutionalization. In a sense, what concepts are to the mind, institutions are to society. They group, they contextualize, they afford a framework for interrelating.

God calls each adult Christian to a personalized lifestyle. The Christian community tends to institutionalize those individual vocations into marriage, celibacy and singlehood. That procedure is both normal and healthy. It becomes a problem, however, when certain people use those institutions as categories into which they try to reduce all the richness and variety of human experience.

Institutions are means, not ends. They are facilitators of understanding, communicating and interrelating. They are not goals in themselves. Each married couple is, therefore, called beyond what the institution of marriage can systematize. Every celibate or single person is challenged to transcend everything that society—whether ecclesial or civil—can possibly formulate or legislate about celibacy or singlehood.

The application of the term "institution" to the three basic vocational lifestyles is clearly analogous. We speak of the "institution of marriage" from both ecclesial and civil viewpoints. Celibacy is much less institutionalized, even in a strictly ecclesial context. Singlehood can hardly be said to be an institution at all.

3) *Models*

Models are related to concepts and institutions. They put flesh and blood on concepts. They personalize the institutions in which we participate. Models are like practical ideals—prototypes, exemplars, paradigms—that we can touch, yet which remain far enough out of our grasp to make us reach for them. Models take what is general and make it concrete. Most people relate more spontaneously to models than they do to concepts or institutions. There are, for example, over a hundred models for Church in the bible: temple (Eph 2:21), living stones (1 Pet 2:5), Body of Christ (Eph 4:12), mustard seed (Mark 4:31), people of God (1 Pet 2:10), etc. The use of models serves a valuable purpose, provided that we remain open to other perspectives.

Throughout this book we use relational models to flesh out the discernment of vocations to marriage, celibacy and singlehood. Each model has the following qualities:

> 1) It is based on divine revelation, but is also derived from observation, reasoning, intuition and common sense.
>
> 2) It exists in relation a) to God who remains the source, the goal and the sustaining force of each vocational lifestyle and b) to creation, both personal and nonpersonal.
>
> 3) It is relative to the sovereign freedom of God as well as to the uniqueness of each person.
>
> 4) It respects the richness of divine mystery and the vastness of human experience.
>
> 5) It matures within an evolutionary perspective. In this life, whatever is relational is also necessarily dynamic and developmental.

Take marriage, for example. The classical model for matrimony combines parental and behavioral models. In that light, marriage is viewed as being for the procreation of children and as a remedy for concupiscence. In the light of a relational model, marriage is perceived as a love-covenant relationship in which each spouse is the principal instrument of God's transforming and purifying activity for the other. Thus, a husband and a wife grow in relatedness to one another, to God and to all creation.

Therefore, in this study when we speak of marriage, celibacy and singlehood, we use concepts, refer to institutions and come out of relational models. In our presentation, however, those vocational designations retain an evolving inner dynamic and a holistic orientation. Those concepts remain in dialogue with faith, having attained some understanding but not complete knowledge. Those institutions remain in interaction with the persons of the Trinity as well as with the infinite variety of people who make up the world. Those models remain relative to God's revelation, to the richness of salvation history and to the variety of human experience.

C. Limitations Linked to Misconceptions about Vocation

Apart from callings to the priesthood and the religious life, many Christian communities have failed to explicitly affirm vocation as a gospel value.[2] This situation has led countless members of those communities to experience a nagging absence of meaning, direction and purpose in life.

A reason for that lack of emphasis has been the mistaken attitude that God chooses certain ones to be priests or religious, while the rest "don't have a vocation." In reality, every human being is specifically called by God,[3] even the stillborn child.

In western societies in particular, the lack of proper emphasis on divine calling as an evangelical value is also related to specific problems stemming from the social environment. These perplexing issues include male-female relationships, enormous economic disparity, vast geographical mobility, incredible technological advancements.[4] As Christians struggle to rethink their values in the light of these developments, they frequently have to face a series of faith crises as well.

A widespread absence of an integrating prayer life[5] in many communities as well as in their individual members contributes greatly to indifference toward vocation as a gospel value. A large number of persons equate their spiritual life primarily with church-going on Sunday and ashes on the first Wednesday of Lent. They reserve a little time for the sacred, but the rest of their lives contains virtually no reference to God. With this attitude, how can vocation receive more than a passing glance?

Only when a person desires to foster an all-embracing relationship with Jesus will vocation become a concern. Only when a community's general level of faith development is such that it values intimate loving communion with Christ will divine calling become a communal value.

[2]See ibid., 136–140.
[3]See ibid., 39–69.
[4]See ibid., 134–136.
[5]See *Contemplation,* 125–140.

D. Limitations Imposed by Insufficient Theologies of Vocation

Anyone entering a process of vocational discernment will have certain assumptions about divine will, providence and calling. Often, those assumptions are unconscious, unexamined and uninformed. When the person operates from unacknowledged premises, s/he usually fails to perceive God-given signs.

A sound theology of vocation is, therefore, a precondition for serious vocational discernment. A challenging theology of vocation helps searching pilgrims to ask the correct questions. A vigorous theology of vocation clears away many illusions and obstacles to listening as it focuses attention on the key issues.

Unfortunately, little substantive material is available regarding the theology of vocation. In our earlier book entitled *Called by God: A Theology of Vocation and Lifelong Commitment,* we present an approach which many find insightful and stimulating. No doubt, other authors will in the future explore other aspects of this mystery.

E. Limitations Caused by a Lack of Direction in Vocational Discernment

Those seeking to discern their vocation need both an attitude of loving receptivity to God and a solid theological framework in which to approach this mystery. Furthermore, it is equally important that they be knowledgeable regarding the practice of discernment. In other words, they must have principles to guide them through their floundering and confusion.

This study addresses directly and at considerable length the principles of discernment for vocations to marriage, celibacy and singlehood.

CHAPTER 4

Principles of Vocational Discernment

The ability to discern a calling to a basic vocational lifestyle is necessary for two fundamental reasons: 1) so that we can cooperate with God ever more consciously and voluntarily in our personal transformation, and 2) so that we can exercise ever more effectively our prophetic mission in the world. Yet, anyone who has undertaken the effort knows how challenging and perplexing vocational discernment can be.

Every discernment process rests on this premise: God manifests God's will both from within us and through the myriad of circumstances which make up our lives.[1]

The Lord effects revelation in many ways: through the Law and the Prophets (Heb 1:1), through the Son (Heb 1:2); through the Church (Matt 28:19-20), through non-Christian religions (Acts 17:22-23; Rom 1:19-20). In recent times, we have come to appreciate more than ever the manifestation of God in and through human experience. Disciplines like psychiatry, developmental psychology, individual and group counseling help us to effectively analyze and synthesize the value of that experience as well as to grow from its lessons.

Thus, God speaks to us in living history. Awareness of the divine will comes to us not only through various belief systems, but also through our needs and aspirations, our joys and struggles, our successes and failures, as well as through our family and community, our friends and enemies, our work and leisure.

[1]See *Spiritual Direction*, 51–94; *Spiritual Journey*, 19–32; *Called by God*, 9–35, 133–140.

A. Principles as Signs along the Faith Journey

It is through faith-imbued reflection on the evolving experience of ourselves and of God within us that we discover our spiritual direction. That personal experience is the starting point for vocational discernment, because it contains within itself the basic principles for discerning vocational lifestyle.

What, then, do we mean by the phrase "principles of vocational discernment"?

The word "principle" denotes a primary source of insight, a comprehensive synthesis of understanding, a concisely formulated guide of conduct. The term "discernment" refers to the faith process whereby we discover something of God's will for us in a particular matter. While many aspects of our faith journey need discerning, our focus in this book is vocation, especially the vocations of marriage, celibacy and singlehood as basic Christian lifestyles.

Principles of vocational discernment are the starting points for reflection on our calling. They are guiding lights in our quest to discover how the Lord is inviting us to become transformed in God. Principles of discernment are not absolute rules or immutable laws governing specific issues. They subtly indicate a way rather than command compliance. They sagaciously point us in a direction rather than dictate a uniform mode of being or action. They enable us to assess possible authenticity.

In diverse situations, principles of discernment are applicable in different ways and in varying degrees. Frequently, these principles contain far more shades of grey than clear black or white. Ordinarily, they imply an element of risk in each application. The main source of these principles is twofold: experience appraised in the light of faith and the vocational lifestyle itself perceived in the light of theological reflection.

An interior calling from God points a person in a direction consistent with that invitation. Movement in that direction gives rise to experiences which prove compatible with the vocation. Out of those experiences flow certain effects or signs which indicate the presence of the particular calling and which authenticate compatibility with its inner dynamics. In that context, signs are observable consequences of an already existing interior reality. These signs constitute what we term "principles of vocational discernment."

> You can tell a tree by its fruit (Luke 6:44).

If we find acorns on a branch, we know that the wood is oak. Therefore, by analogy and in faith, certain signs indicate a possible calling to marriage, while others point to celibacy and still others to singlehood.

Everyone's vocation is utterly unique. Nonetheless, when we observe a number of persons called to a given lifestyle, we notice also certain signs which are common to their experiences. Obviously, those signs exist in varying degrees and with widely differing nuances. Yet, commonalities persist. Those commonalities form the nucleus of principles of discernment.

These principles, in turn, serve as guidelines which help us discover something of God's will. The Lord deals with each of us in a wholly personal manner. Yet, as God has established laws in nature, so too God has fashioned certain patterns in the spiritual life. These patterns remain flexible, and their application is tailored to individual callings. Yet, these patterns possess a universal quality. They exist more or less in most, if not all, similar cases. Some principles are merely signs along the way. Other principles express procedures and processes which enable us to arrive at a better understanding of God's mysterious workings within us.

We must distinguish principles of discernment from discernment itself. Principles are the signs, the guidelines, the formulas, the methods, the models, the maxims, the propositions which both reflect and embody a key element of reality as it relates to the process of discernment. Discernment, on the other hand, is the spiritual understanding which God imparts through faith (Col 1:9; 1 Cor 2:10-14). No amount of principles equals discernment. We humans formulate principles out of the light of our intelligence and experience. Only God can produce discernment—that is, the faith interpretation of that intelligence and experience.

All true discernment unfolds within the darkness and commitment of faith.[2] Surrender in faith enables the discerning pilgrim not only to perceive God's signs but also to interpret the

[2]See *O Blessed Night*, 89–94, 147–151; *Receptivity*, 49–53, 97–101; *Spiritual Journey*, 173–180.

way the Spirit is leading. Thus, faith illumines us with some understanding of our vocation. Faith impels us to risk moving into the unknown and to embark upon the way which God seems to be indicating. Faith calls us to live out our vocation in ever deeper faith.

In actual discernment, faith enlightens us through the merging of our intuition and common sense. Intuition pierces beyond logic and reasoning to attain the core of the reality at hand. In a sense, intuition transcends time, space and processes in order to get to the naked truth of the matter. Common sense, on the other hand, relates the findings of intuition not only to the here and now, but also to everything around us. Common sense applies intuition to concrete life with all its ramifications. When in faith we grasp something intuitively and our practical wisdom confirms it, we can be confident that the direction thus indicated indeed approximates God's will for us, at least for the moment.

Persons of prayer and faith rarely err when intuition and common sense converge on a particular issue. Frequently, however, in order to complete the picture they need to search out further aspects of the truth from other sources. A young woman, for example, may know intuitively that God is calling her to marriage, and her common sense may confirm that direction. Yet, the question of specifically whom to wed may still be unresolved. Many vocations also require communal discernment and a calling from the community.[3] All that discernment requires time, dialogue and mutual openness.

B. The Focus of Vocational Discernment

In the development of vocational consciousness, there are sequential phases.[4]

The most primitive of these is characterized by conformity to the established Christian order. That phase is usually followed by one in which vocational consciousness is redefined in the light of personal relationships with God and significant others. Out of that advancement eventually emerges a third

[3]See *Called by God,* 137–139.

[4]See ibid., 99–112, 141–150.

phase of vocational awareness: calling experienced as an existential inability to be, become and do otherwise. This third phase coincides with the interior readiness to begin a lifelong commitment.[5]

In this study, that third phase is the primary context in which we formulate the principles for discerning possible vocations to marriage and celibacy. We treat also the principles for discerning a possible calling to singlehood, whether a vocational imperative or only a general awareness is operative. Thus, the pilgrim whom we envisage is advancing toward explicit consciousness of an existential inability to become otherwise. In the case of marriage or celibacy, the Christian is already moving voluntarily forward in the direction of lifelong commitment.

At that threshold of vocational consciousness, the presence of a specific calling reveals itself in certain observable signs and effects. These indications are not only signs, but also conditions. That is, unless they are present it would be folly to presume the existence of a vocation to marriage or celibacy at this time.

While we focus primarily on the principles of discernment which authenticate a particular vocation once the individual's awareness has reached the threshold of an existential inability, we recognize that this threshold is but the climax of a lengthy process of listening and searching. The presence of a vocation is born into consciousness after a long gestation. As the process takes its course and as mature vocational awareness emerges, the signs become more observable. In the case of marriage and celibacy, the impulse toward lifelong commitment also intensifies. The long process of discernment requires testing of the signs until the discernee experiences vocational maturity. The pilgrim must refrain from putting premature closure on the work which God is accomplishing.

Vocational consciousness, in the sense of existential inability, may precede or coincide with the celebration of the sacrament of matrimony or the ritualization of celibacy. Yet, many persons come to this experiential discovery of their calling long after pronouncing their vows. In these instances, their true vo-

[5]See ibid., 115–132.

cation does not always coincide with the one they had anticipated.

The existential inability to become otherwise is *God's* ultimate sign and condition of authenticity for an individual vocation. Spiritual directors, pastors, counselors, superiors, prospective spouses, aspirants, formation personnel, etc. have an obligation to wait out the birthing process—no matter how long it takes. Nuptials *ráta et consummáta* do not of themselves constitute or confirm a vocation from God to marry a particular person. Nor does the canonical profession of a vow of chastity or celibacy automatically mean that God has called that individual to a celibate lifestyle.

Ideally, nuptials or professions should sacramentalize or solemnize an already existing call by God. Experience, however, teaches that such is not always the case. What happens, then, when a man realizes that he has married the "wrong" woman or when a nun realizes that she has made the "wrong" vow? A direct response to those questions of conscience does not fall explicitly within the scope of this book. Yet, many of the principles which we offer contribute to an enlightened resolution of those situations.

The focus of this study is those principles of discernment which bear directly upon authenticating a person's existential inability, whenever it occurs in his/her life. These principles are both general and detailed. They remain "general" because they are generally applicable to similar lifestyles. These principles are also "detailed," because those discerning, together with their spiritual guides, need to grasp them thoroughly if they hope to relate them properly to personal experience. Cursory overviews of these principles do not as a rule suffice for accurate interpretation in actual living situations.

MARRIED LIFE

CHAPTER 5

Marriage: A Mutual Sacramental Consecration

Jesus, referring in part to a statement in the second account of creation (Gen 2:24), teaches the rudiments of a calling to matrimony and furnishes the fundamental principles to discern its authenticity:

> A man will leave his father and mother
> and be united to his wife,
> and the two will become one . . .
> Therefore, what God has united,
> let no one separate (Matt 19:5-6).

The vocation to marriage in effect comprises two callings: one, to matrimony in general as a basic lifestyle; the other, to marriage with a specific person as one's life-partner. Thus, God invites a man and a woman to commit themselves in love to each other and to God in the context of a conjugal way of life until the death of one of them.

The Lord calls the couple to participate intimately in one another's journey with Christ to the Father in the Spirit. As individuals, God calls each spouse to personal transforming union. As a couple, God calls both spouses to participate directly in one another's deification. Because of their mutual vocation to Christian marriage, a couple experiences a need to share in a unique manner both themselves and their way of life with each other. They need to journey together to the Father in a union so close and so intimate that they will henceforth engage in a shared covenanted life. A man and a woman, both as individuals and as a couple, celebrate their consecration to Christ in the sacrament of matrimony.

The vocation to married life encompasses a threefold consecration. God makes a husband and wife holy in three interrelated ways. 1) By virtue of the grace celebrated in baptism and confirmation, God has already consecrated each of them to God. In matrimony the Lord deepens that consecration by enabling both spouses to intensify their relationship with the Trinity. 2) In matrimony the spouses also consecrate themselves to each other. They declare before God and society that they need to let God sanctify the one through the other: the husband through the wife and the wife through the husband. 3) In marriage God consecrates them specifically as a couple—as "one"—to God.

From a pastoral viewpoint, study and discussion of the theology and the psychology of matrimony are essential aspects of Christian formation. Catechetical instruction must focus on the spiritual dimensions of the sacrament, the nature and gift of human love, the dynamics of interpersonal communication, the stages of married life, etc. Since those themes refer to primary Christian and human values, they have to be included in each Christian's education.

Those topics remain important for everyone, regardless of lifestyle. Yet, when viewed in the context of contemplating a specific marital partner, they assume new meaning and urgency. In our development of this section on married life, we address precisely this situation. We highlight the principles for discerning a vocation to marry a particular person. Most of these principles are also relevant to the discernment of a call to matrimony in general.

A. Consciousness of a Call to Christian Marriage

When a person becomes conscious of a possible calling to sacramental marriage, this awareness occurs in either of two contexts: On the one hand, the prospective spouses may be single. On the other hand, one or both may be involved in a legally binding marriage, but a "marriage" which one or both now discern as not from God. In other words, a person married prior to having experienced an authentic vocational imperative to do so, and his/her vocational awareness indicates now that the premature marital commitment was a mistake.[1]

Many single persons become aware of a general calling to matrimony as a way of life prior to meeting their God-intended spouses. They consciously desire to marry eventually, to settle down someday and possibly to raise a family. Frequently, that vocational awareness develops through a series of passing amorous relationships. It may persist for years before the right partner comes along. Other single persons find that explicit consciousness of their vocation to a wedded lifestyle coincides with the awakening of their desire to marry a specific person.

It is primarily in the second instance that a desire for matrimony as a way of life undergoes its acid test. Contemplating marriage with a particular individual forces the two persons to focus directly on the possibility of a mutual vocation. If the man and the woman possess sufficient vocational maturity, they will ask questions to this effect: Is God calling us to wed each other? Is this person the spouse whom the Lord intends for me? Am I ready to marry him/her now? Are there positive signs that our union will endure for the rest of our mortal lives?

Confronted with those questions, however, many couples together with their spiritual advisors do not know how to formulate the principles necessary to guide their discernment.

When the intended spouses are single, the discernment is tedious enough. But, when a person is in a legally binding marriage and yet believes that s/he is called to wed someone else, the discernment can be immeasurably more complex.

A major obstacle to marital discernment is the lack of recognition by many people of marriage—whether in general or with a specific person—as a vocation. Some view marriage as something that they are expected to do eventually. Others see it purely as an option which they can make or not, now or in the future. God does not enter the picture until much later in their lives, if at all. The awareness of an existential inability to be other than married (and *a fortiori* wedded to this person) all too frequently does not occur until long after the nuptials.

[1]See *Called by God,* 108–111, 122–130.

In reality, the commitments implied in such marriages are premature. The exchange of vows has preceded the explicit consciousness within the couple of a God-given calling to a lifelong covenant.

Nevertheless, the inner dynamics of an authentic vocation can be at work without these persons adverting to the fact. The man and the woman who are prematurely married may eventually realize that theirs has always been a marriage made in heaven, so to speak. They had happily made the correct choice from the outset, although they did so without realizing the extent to which God was influencing their decision. When this couple does reach mature vocational awakening, their conjugal life becomes more qualitatively and spiritually meaningful. Two spouses can arrive at that awareness separately and at different times. It may, for example, dawn clearly on one partner after a few years, but only vaguely and after several decades on the other.

Many couples, however, realize that their premature nuptials were a mistake. At some point they begin to question whether God has indeed called them to spend the rest of their lives together. The fact that one or both are amorously involved with someone else may or may not occasion that awareness. Even when love of a third-party is at issue, that love does not automatically imply a vocation to marry the other. In some cases third-party involvement is a way of evading, rather than working through, marital difficulties which are resolvable. In other marriages third-party involvement is a means of jolting a spouse into facing a longstanding but unrecognized problem. Attraction to a third-party could also be an invitation to a nonconjugal relationship with the other. The possible vocation to marry someone else is a very difficult discernment. It requires deep faith, prolonged searching and soul-wrenching honesty.

We begin our reflections on the principles for the discernment of a vocation to marriage by considering the starting point of all vocational awareness: the mystery of divine calling. We address our discussion primarily to Christian couples preparing to respond to their call. However, the principles of discernment in this and in the following six chapters are applicable, *mutátis mutándis,* to couples already married in some sense who are seeking to discern whether God is calling them to remain together. In this section on marriage, we prescind from discussing what is referred to as "domestic partnerships," whether heterosexual or homosexual.[2]

B. The Mystery of a Divine Calling to Marriage

Each vocation is mysterious. The vocation which a man and a woman receive to marry each other is doubly so. Indeed, "it is a great mystery" (Eph 5:32).

Why God calls two people to marry one another rather than any number of others whom each might find desirable and in some ways even preferable, is utterly beyond reason. Why they are impelled to enter into a lifelong partnership of conjugal love with each other to the exclusion of all others is logically inexplicable. A happily married couple may be able to give some explanation: certain appealing qualities in the beloved, similar goals in life, physical attraction, etc. Ultimately, however, they readily acknowledge the existence in their mutual choice of something which transcended all rationale. That reason beyond all reason was (and still is) God's call to be united in love to each other in matrimony. The "I-don't-know-what"[3] which drew them together was in fact a unique participation in divine *agápe.*

Fundamentally, a couple recognize their vocation to marry by faith-imbued intuition and common sense. That intuition is the wisdom which flows from love of God and of each other. It is the insight which arises from hope in God and in one another. Common sense in this context denotes practical assessment of the situation. Having weighed both positive and negative influences, the marriage mysteriously makes sense to the couple in terms of how they are to become themselves in Christ Jesus.

Encountering the mystery of one another, a man and a woman experience God calling them to share every facet of themselves for as long as they both shall live. For some couples, love happens at first sight. For most couples, however,

[2]See ibid., 130–132.

[3]St. John of the Cross, *The Spiritual Canticle,* stanza 7.

it develops through lengthy maturation. In either instance the prospective spouses come to the awareness of having attained sufficient stature in Christ to share together the rest of their lives. They see that in doing so they will receive their holiness, peace, freedom and personal fulfillment. If theirs is an authentic calling to marriage, both a man and a woman will eventually recognize their mutual vocational imperative, but not necessarily at the same time or with identical intensity.

C. Sense of Vocation versus Projective Identification

The intuitive recognition which flows from a divine calling to marriage differs radically from the mutual attraction experienced in what certain psychologists term "projective identification."[4]

At least initially, projective identification entails mutual idealization on the part of a man and a woman. The couple become caught up in the fantasy that each will fulfill all the other's longings, satisfy all unmet needs, actualize all romantic dreams. These persons are under the illusion that each will complete the other in every respect. By means of that idealization, the couple trick themselves into a relationship wherein unresolved inner conflicts are bound to flare up and demand resolution.

When projective identification occurs, a satisfying sense of the familiar initially draws the couple together. "What is 'right', when it comes to the choosing of a mate, is to some degree what has been and what is familiar; it is what 'works' on that inner template, or pattern of assumptions about what an intimate partnership is like."[5]

That sense of the familiar has its roots deep in the past. Projective identification springs from unresolved conflict related to childhood or adolescent experiences with parents or

[4]See Maggie Scarf, *Intimate Partners: Patterns in Love and Marriage* (New York: Random House, 1987) 3–100, 359–375; Augustus Napier, *The Fragile Bond: In Search of an Equal, Intimate and Enduring Marriage* (New York: Harper & Row, 1988) 207–274; A. Napier, *The Family Crucible* (New York: Harper & Row, 1985) 45–49, 147–161.

[5]Scarf, *Intimate Partners*, 79.

family. Each partner unconsciously seeks to reenact and to resolve those past experiences in a current relationship with the other partner who has a complementary inner conflict. Together the couple unwittingly create a context in which each tries to relive a past relationship and to make it turn out right this time around. For example, the woman may be unknowingly seeking from her mate the closeness she still craves from her unaffectionate father. Perhaps the man is unconsciously still trying to distance himself from a doting mother. Thus, the two partners in collusion project their intrapsychic conflicts on one another.

Two people caught in the vortex of projective identification tend to be at roughly the same emotional level of development. The qualities which first attracted them to each other are the key to identifying the specific intrapsychic conflicts projected into the relationship. Moreover, these qualities also become with time the principal sources of conflict in the relationship. What each at first perceived positively in the other, s/he later reinterprets and renames in an unfavorable light. This reversal begins when the couple's idealization of each other starts to clash with reality.

Projective identification operates primarily in two ways: 1) in a literal restaging of the past, or 2) in a more subtle reenactment of a familial situation.

An example of the first would be the child of an alcoholic parent who as an adult chooses a spouse who is also an alcoholic. An example of the second would be the man who transposes into a current relationship his family of origin's system for being intimate. The man functions by using what is familiar. The fact that other modes of intimacy exist does not occur to him because he remains blindly locked into the system internalized within his family. Suppose that this man had a father who failed to succeed in his career and a mother who was disgusted with the father. The man may unconsciously repeat through various strategies what he learned in early life about male-female relationships. Having done so, he may find himself one day unable to reach a major goal in his chosen field and burdened with a wife who rejects him for it.

Projective identification entails an unconsciously-motivated interaction in which two partners in collusion use each other to experience and to contain certain split-off dimensions of themselves. Each partner is assigned, takes on and expresses some of the other's denied or repressed emotions, feelings, wishes or attitudes. Each sees aspects of him/herself in the other, but without realizing that these qualities or feelings actually exist within him/herself.

Projective identification as a defense mechanism enables the partners to alter their self-image and at the same time to modify their perceptions of one another. Take, for instance, a couple whose projective identification centers around a conflict between autonomy and intimacy. These two persons are unable to appreciate that each needs both autonomy and intimacy. The man sees himself as self-sufficient, and tends to deny his need for closeness. The woman wants intimacy, but is unaware of her latent longing for independence. When the man wants intimacy, he experiences that desire as existing in his partner rather than in himself. When the woman needs distance, she perceives that wish as coming from her mate rather than as originating in her. In this situation, the man depends on the woman to pursue him when he desires closeness. She, on the other hand, depends on him to run when she chases, thereby establishing space to satisfy her unrecognized need for autonomy. One sends out to the other the appropriate vibes, which the other unconsciously perceives and acts upon.

In the long run, instead of furnishing mutual fulfillment projective identification leaves a couple confused and frustrated. Each partner ends up fighting against and disapproving of the precise needs, feelings or attitudes assigned to his/her mate in the initial collusive bargain. Thus, they experience the complex of attractions that drew them together in the first place as a tangle of irreconcilable differences.

D. Authentic Vocational Awareness

How can we discern whether a divine calling rather than projective identification is drawing a couple to marry?

A *first sign* authenticating a sense of vocation is a realistic attitude on the part of each partner toward his/her childhood and adolescent years. Mutual exploration of their respective family histories can be an enlightening experience for a couple considering marriage. Of particular significance are the nature of the two family systems and the evolution of relationships with their respective parents and siblings. Reconstruction of each partner's family tree can assist in this respect. A genogram helps shed light on the behavioral patterns which the partners bring to their relationship. The couple thus gain knowledge of the modes of thinking, feeling and acting which they have inherited from their past and which they are likely to repeat with each other.[6] A realistic assessment of family history consists in explicit recognition of the joy and pain, the affirmation and deprivation, the harmony and conflicts of growing up. Moreover, basic reconciliation of the man and the woman with their respective families of origin bespeaks a maturity which in turn facilitates the emergence of a sense of vocation.

An appropriate balance of opposites within each partner constitutes a *second sign* of authentic vocational awareness. Each person needs to have integrated to some degree the seemingly contradictory dimensions of personhood: autonomy and intimacy, dependence and independence, union with others and personal uniqueness, feelings and logic, etc. This balance indicates the existence of the basic psychological, emotional and spiritual maturity which is ordinarily a prerequisite for vocational awareness. As maturity increases, so too does self-knowledge. That emerging insight gives rise in turn to a need to periodically readjust the balance of opposites.

A *third sign* of genuine vocational awareness consists in realistic expectations of each other and of the relationship itself. Contemporary psychological research and pastoral experience indicate that many couples enter marriage much too idealistically. Some researchers speak of the early stages of marriage as a movement from idealization to disenchantment to productivity.[7] Others describe the pattern as a shift from fantasy to compromise to reality.[8] Those researchers describe marriage as it currently unfolds in our society. The question we

[6]See ibid., 7–8, 40–71.

[7]See ibid., 14.

[8]See for example Maxine Rock, *The Marriage Map: Understanding and Surviving the Stages of Marriage* (Atlanta: Peachtree Publishers, 1986) 38–151.

pose is this: Is there not a more mature starting point for a lifelong commitment than such idealization and fantasy?

We believe that a more solid beginning is not only possible but also necessary. The crux of that foundation is mature vocational awareness and competent spiritual guidance. The presence of these two factors encourages reality-orientatedness in a couple during courtship and even more so during engagement.

With the proper spiritual guidance the couple develop awareness both individually and as a unit not only of their attractive qualities but also of their limitations and weaknesses. Thus, they identify the areas in which they can reasonably expect improvement as well as those where change is unlikely. While acknowledging what they share in common, the couple recognize also the impact of their differences upon the relationship. Without realistic knowledge of one another, they wed an illusion rather than a person.

Some projective identification occurs in the initial phases of most intimate relationships. Its occurrence is not entirely negative. In fact, this dynamic can become a catalyst for growth. Having been repeatedly frustrated by the failure to live up to each other's expectations, a couple may reach a crisis point wherein they are willing to let go their illusions and face up to the woundedness incurred in their families of origin. Inner healing and movement toward wholeness are then possible, and one becomes capable of seeing the other as s/he truly is.

Thus, in a relationship where projective identification does occur, a call to marriage is still possible. However, couples would usually have to be well into the process of working through that defense mechanism before signs of an authentic vocation become discernible. Until then, they lack the freedom and knowledge necessary for mature vocational commitment. When projective identification exists without a divine calling to marriage, the relationship ceases when one or both partners resolve the issue. Nothing remains to hold the couple together.

A sense of vocation to marriage arises from God abiding within the two persons. It consists in a mysterious yet undeniable conviction that the Lord is leading them to share their life together until death. A couple cannot have, nor can any spiritual guide furnish them, proof of a God-given calling to marriage. They make their choice of each other in faith. Moreover, the celebration of that choice in the sacrament of matrimony, as well as the daily living out of that commitment, is an ongoing and deepening act of faith, hope and love in each other as well as in God. Unconditional surrender to each other and to their unknown future together is integral to their vocation:

> For better or for worse,
> for richer or for poorer,
> in sickness and in health,
> until death do you part (The Rite of Matrimony).

Thus, a sense of vocation, together with an appreciation for the mystery of divine calling, is a first principle for discerning whether a couple's desire to marry is from God. From a theological viewpoint, a couple's entry into a sacramental marriage appropriately occurs only after the attainment of that threshold of mystery, that sense of personal vocation and that experience of mutual existential inability to become otherwise. Without those qualities, the sacrament cannot adequately symbolize the reality which it is meant to signify. Something essential would be lacking in the couple's ability to consent to the marriage and to make a lifelong commitment to each other and to God.

CHAPTER 6

Love: The Vocational Basis for Marriage

For a Christian, the choice of a marital partner is a matter of mystery—the mystery of an utterly gratuitous divine calling. And, at the very core of that mystery is the gift of love.

All essential aspects of marriage as a sacrament converge upon love. Conjugal love is a sign of Christ's intimate love for his Church (Eph 5:21-33). Commitment in love between a husband and a wife is the symbol of the Lord's unremitting love for each of God's people. Growth in love between spouses is a unique embodiment of the Lord's transforming and purifying love for every person.

The presence of mutual love is a crucial indication that a man and a woman's choice of each other may be flowing from a vocation to matrimony. Love is the foundation of the marital covenant and of lifelong commitment in marriage. Discernment thus has to address the issue of the authenticity and the quality of the couple's love.

A. Capacity for Self-Love

Usually, our capacity to love another human being, or even God, depends on our ability to love ourselves sufficiently and correctly. Ordinarily, our capacity to be at home with someone else is proportionate to our ability to be at home with ourselves. Rudiments of that truth were already present in the Levitical code:

Love your neighbor as yourself (Lev 19:18, 34).

The same standard is reemphasized by Jesus (Matt 19:19, 22:39), reiterated by Paul (Rom 13:9; Gal 5:14) and restated by James (Jas 2:8).

Healthy self-love, therefore, is a precondition for intimacy with others. This principle is so evident from human experience and general psychology that we will not belabor it here.

B. Spouses Called to Love One Another

To love suggests giving freely, joyfully and tenderly of oneself to another. To love denotes wanting to share intimately with someone and desiring that the person reciprocate in kind. To love implies longing to be with the other physically, emotionally, spiritually. To love connotes indwelling the beloved and delighting in communion with him/her.

Yet, there is love and there is "love." There is loving and there is "making love." There is being-in-love and there is "falling in and out of love." In contemporary English, we have many expressions to nuance our use and abuse of affection.

The English language has also a variety of words and phrases which indicate a certain qualitative gradation in the fervor and glow of human affection. This progression can be situated along a continuum of intensity. People express this sequence with verbs, nouns and adjectives. From among that rich variety of expressions, we choose a succession of words and phrases to highlight key developments along the continuum. We use these words and phrases in the ordinary sense that most people understand them. No doubt, these expressions have diverse suppositions in various parts of the English-speaking world. Even within an individual's life, each term can have several meanings. Yet, what is important in our presentation is not so much the words themselves, but the sense of progression and the thresholds of intensity that we associate with them.

Both our capacity to be loved and our ability to love are infinite. The more love participates in *agápe,* the more it approaches pure quality. Yet, this side of the resurrection, we remain immersed in space and time. In this mortal condition, we tend not only to measure everything quantitatively but also to conceptualize and to speak of purely qualitative realities quantitatively. Although, strictly speaking, love cannot be measured, understanding its progress and expressing our experience of its intensification remain important. Thus, in relation to progression in loving, people say that they love and are loved "more and more." Even though "more" denotes quantity, it bespeaks as well a certain qualitative intensification. It is that movement toward purer and purer quality that we wish to describe through the following verbs, nouns and adjectives.

1) *Verbs Suggesting Progression in Loving*

Even though we present this continuum of affection in the context of a divine calling to marriage, the basic dynamics of intensifying love are universal. That is, something of this experience is perceived in our relationship with God as well as with people, in instances of celibate love as well as of single love.

We identify six degrees of intensity along the continuum of affection. We present them in an order which proceeds from the least intense toward the most intense. Six verbs typical of intensifying affection are: *liking* someone, *enjoying the company* of another, *caring for* an individual, *truly loving* a person, *tenderly loving* someone and *being-in-love* with another.

Not every affective relationship runs the gamut of all six phases. Indeed, most relationships do not pass through more than one or two phases. There is such a thing as love-at-first-sight. Thus, an affection can begin at an advanced degree and could increase or decrease in intensity along the continuum. Sometimes, people believe initially that they are in-love, but as time passes and familiarity sets in, they discover that they just like each other or enjoy one another's company.

Most of us like many people. Some of these we like more, others less. The people we like affect us positively, but usually they pass with ease in and out of our life. Their influence is often dependent on physical proximity. That is: If they are present, that's fine; and, if they are absent, that's equally acceptable.

Enjoying another's company takes liking that person up a notch. In this case, we deliberately seek out the other in order to take pleasure in his/her presence. If for some reason that person is not available, we are disappointed.

Caring for an individual signals a further step along the continuum. We are not referring to caretaking or caregiving in a managerial or a clinical sense. Rather, we are speaking of the sentiment expressed in the statement "I care a great deal for you." Some people use that phrase to signify "I almost love you." Frequently, these people cannot quite say "I love you" or cannot quite mean it. Caring for someone in this manner indicates a threshold in the intensification of positive regard because the other person now makes a significant difference in our life. Thus, caring for a person connotes having warm affection for him/her and ordinarily marks the beginning of intimacy in a relationship.

Actually loving a person is the next threshold along the continuum. In the context of marriage, this is a most critical threshold in the progression of affection since it is inconceivable that God would call two persons into this sacramental covenant without also gifting them with true love for each other. Whatever liking, enjoying or caring for someone may mean, truly loving a person denotes direct participation with the other in divine *agápe*. Marital love is more than giving oneself freely, joyfully and intimately to one's spouse. It is also God in one partner communing lovingly with God in the other. This threshold is a minimum requirement in the discernment of a vocation to marry a particular person. We say "minimum" because there are at least two further possible degrees of intensification: loving "tenderly" and being-in-love.

True love for another—whether in marriage or apart from it—is a participation in divine *agápe*. Just as *agápe* is everlasting, so too is true love. To love truly is to love forever. Once this gift is received and this threshold of affection is crossed, what is of *agápe* in the love endures.

We must note, however, that the love between two spouses differs in uniqueness from the New Testament's general mandate to love everyone: our enemies (Matt 5:44), our neighbor (Luke 10:27-37), one another (John 15:17), each brother and sister (1 John 4-20), etc. A Christian's love of all persons is truly a participation in God's love for all (John 3:16; 1 John 4:7-17). But the love of one spouse for another is a unique sacramental participation in Christ's love for his Church.

The distinction between truly (or simply) loving and tenderly (or dearly) loving is primarily one of degree. No new threshold as such is crossed. The difference is often one of feeling and enthusiasm. Thus, to say "I love you tenderly" or "I dearly love you" tends to express a warmth and an excitement not necessarily implied in the phrase "I love you." Yet, from another point of view, "I love you" says it all.

Being-in-love with a person is the ultimate participation in divine *agápe* in this life. It is also the ultimate threshold along the continuum of affection. We take up this subject in the next chapter.

According to the above six expressions of intensity in affection, any one of us may love but a handful of persons during the course of life. Of those, we may love dearly or tenderly two or three. Not everyone is blessed to be-in-love with someone. Because of woundedness, dysfunctionality or other influences, not everyone is capable of this intensity of love. Yet, when an individual is so gifted, the experience rarely occurs more than once in a lifetime.

2) *Nouns Indicating Progression in Love*

The term "friend" covers a multitude of situations and relationships. Using friendship as a basic point of reference, we offer several noun phrases which approximate the six verbs mentioned above: a *casual friend,* a *good friend,* a *close friend,* a *very special friend,* an *inseparable friend,* the *beloved friend.* All the qualifying adjectives are relative, but depending on intention and inflection they can express a gradual intensification of affection in a relationship.

Someone I like I may call "a casual friend." Someone whose company I enjoy and seek out I might call "a good friend." Someone I really care for I am apt to call "a close friend."

Once the threshold of true love is crossed, however, the intensity of friendship becomes qualitatively transformed. The words "very special" and "inseparable" catch something of this progression in the contexts of loving truly and loving tenderly. Those who are in-love attain an ultimate threshold in the unique interchange of lover and beloved. Each lover becomes the other's beloved friend. Rarely in life is a person in-love with more than one human being.

3) *Adjectives Associated with Progression in Love*

Three adjectives in particular describe something of the typical sentiments related to the various intensities of loving. They are: *affectionate, romantic* and *passionate.*

Ordinarily, we speak of affection toward persons we enjoy being around and especially toward those for whom we care. Part of us goes out to them. Usually, along with affection we experience romantic sentiments toward those we truly or tenderly love. We feel amorous and are utterly devoted to them. Spontaneously, we associate passionate with being-in-love. This ultimate intensity of loving is an all-consuming fire that purifies as it transforms lover in beloved.

Whether we use adjectives, nouns or verbs, the words we employ are like colors in a spectrum. We can sometimes see the difference between them, but looking more closely each blends imperceptibly into the other. Yet, unlike a spectrum which can be static, the continuum of affection is always shifting.

4) *Schema of the Continuum of Affection*

The following is a résumé—using typical verbs, nouns and adjectives—of the six phases of intensifying affection. We highlight the three critical thresholds.

liking	enjoying	*caring for*	*loving truly*	loving tenderly	*being-in-love with*
a casual friend	a good friend	a *close friend*	a *very special friend*	an inseparable friend	a *beloved friend*
	affectionate		*romantic*		*passionate*

In summary, a crucial sign that God may be calling a man and a woman to marriage is the discernment that each has reached at least the threshold of truly loving the other. They are at a minimum very special friends, and they are drawn to a romantic exchange of their mutual love.

CHAPTER 7

Love for Each Other

A calling to Christian marriage entails necessarily the gift of true love between a man and a woman. That gift constitutes a special participation in *agápe.*

The New Testament authors use the word *agápe* to reveal something of the love which exists between Father, Son and Spirit; the love with which God loves us; the love with which we love God and one another in God. The Letter to the Colossians applies that love to marriage:

> Husbands, love [*agapáte*] your wives (Col 3:19).

Of all the signs indicating a possible vocation to matrimony, none is more significant than the authenticity and the quality of the couple's love. The sacrament of Christian marriage has as its foundation God's calling of two persons to witness divine transforming love in a specific manner and the Lord's calling of them to a lifelong covenant in love. Thus, at the very core of this vocation is love of husband and wife for one another.

A. The Letter to the Ephesians on Marital Love

The author of the Letter to the Ephesians insists on this general mandate to all Christians:

> Be submissive to one another
> out of reverence for Christ (Eph 5:21).

In a society which stresses dialogue, collective bargaining and collegial decision-making, submissiveness is not a generally welcomed concept. Nonetheless, when submissiveness is understood in the sense of mutual acquiescence, respect, malleability—approaching one another in meekness, humility and gentleness—it is an evangelical value and a Christian virtue.

Having stated the general mandate to extend deference to one another, the text from Ephesians goes on to apply that instruction to the particular situation of wives in relation to their husbands:

> Wives, submit to your husbands
> as to the Lord . . .
> As the church submits to Christ,
> so also wives should submit to their husbands (Eph 5:22, 24).

Whatever the text's understanding of submission, the author of Ephesians compares a wife's rapport to her husband with her rapport "to the Lord," "to Christ." In other words, a wife's relationship with her husband in Christian marriage is patterned on the imitation of her relationship with Christ, the Lord. In the light of the gospel the crux of that relationship can be none other than love, *agápe.*

The author of Ephesians is even more explicit regarding the importance of love on the part of a husband for his wife. We arrange the following three passages in a qualitatively progressive sequence.

> Husbands ought to love their wives
> as their own bodies . . .
> which they nourish and cherish
> as Christ does the church (Eph 5:28-29).

> Each one of you husbands must love his wife
> as he loves himself (Eph 5:33).

> Husbands, love your wives,
> just as Christ loved the Church
> and gave himself up for her
> to make her holy (Eph 5:25-26).

Among those three passages, there is a unifying theme: love. Each text repeats the verb *agapáo.* The sense is this: Love in its deepest evangelical sense (*agápe*) lies at the core of a Christian husband's covenant with his wife. Reverence for her and attentiveness to her needs are not of themselves sufficient to enter into marriage. However, when true love is present, then reverence, attentiveness, affection, respect, etc. ensue.

Following the sequence of the texts cited above, the comparisons imply a subtle progression in the intensity of love:

- *as they love their own bodies,* which they nourish and cherish in a wholistic Christian way;
- *as they love themselves,* that is, their deepest inner selves where God abides in them and they abide in God;
- *as Christ himself loves his church,* which he does to the point of actually giving himself up for her that she may participate in his own holiness, his divinity.

Concerning the last comparison, Jesus reveals elsewhere the unimaginable depths of his love for the church and for each one of us:

> Greater love [*agápe*] than this no one has
> than to lay down one's life . . . (John 15:13).

B. Being-in-Love

Truly loving one another suffices for a calling to Christian marriage. For some couples, however, their participation in *agápe* is so deep that they are in-love with each other.

What does it mean to be-in-love?

Clearly, that expression does not refer to infatuation: the falling in and out of amorous relationships. Neither does it denote the psychological phenomenon of projecting one's animus or anima on another. Nor does it indicate addiction to someone or codependent behavior by a couple. Furthermore, it does not connote romantic involvement per se, although romance is frequently present when two persons are in-love.

Rather, we use the phrase "being-in-love" in the spiritual sense of unconditional commitment in love of one's deepest self to that which is deepest and most mysterious in the beloved. Being-in-love implies a mutual indwelling, a radical faith in one another and an unshakable hope in each other. This intensity of love can exist between persons of the same or opposite sex. It can exist especially in relation to God.

Being-in-love is impossible to describe in rational, logical and *a fortiori* juridical terms. Yet, the experience is undeniable for the person undergoing it. Individuals in-love know it in every fiber of their being.

When two people are in-love, they become one in affective communion. They listen to and empathize spontaneously with each other. They participate in each other's way of seeing, thinking, feeling, all the while maintaining their respective individualities. They share hopes and aspirations, disappointments and setbacks. They experience an affinity of hearts, minds and spirits. So intimate is their communion that the lover somehow abides in the beloved and the beloved mysteriously lives in the lover.

In the expression "to be-in-love," the verb "to be" emphasizes enduring and ever intensifying mutual indwelling. The couple's loving communion continues even when they are not directly feeling love for or thinking of each other.

The noun "love" means gift of self. To be "in-love" denotes the giving of one's *whole* self to the other—with all one's energy, heart and spirit. The gift of all one's self enhances the individuality of both the lover and the beloved even as it intensifies the union of the two. Yet, this side of the resurrection there remains a certain relativity to that gift. One gives oneself to the beloved to the degree that one possesses a self that can be shared. That self is always developing. Thus, the following truth obtains:

> I love you more today than yesterday,
> but still less than I shall tomorrow.

Being-in-love produces profound integration within the lover. Love for the beloved channels one's physical, psychological, emotional and sexual energies. The more holistic that integration, the greater the capacity for fidelity. Fidelity flows from and is commensurate with the intensity of love, since lovers can be only as faithful as they love. For couples in-love, fidelity is second-nature.

In this life love cannot unite without at the same time purifying. As love draws two people into communion, each dies to selfishness in receiving the other and in surrendering self to the other. Being-in-love purifies in two ways: 1) Love gradually empties lovers of egocentricity. 2) Love progressively wounds[1] the lovers with an irresistible longing to love each other more perfectly. Love yearns for ever deeper affection and more fulfilling union. Love's inner dynamics give rise to a longing in the lovers to be completely one, but without being swallowed up by each other.

Being-in-love enables two persons to encounter what is deepest and most mysterious in one another. Each realizes that there is infinitely more of the beloved to be known, experienced, revealed. This love fills them with wonder before the inexhaustible ever unfolding mystery of one another's personhood.

The encounter with what is deepest and most ineffable in each other draws lovers beyond themselves. Through one another's finite being, God opens their hearts to the infinite. Through each other's creatureliness, the Lord opens their hearts to the uncreated.[2] Being-in-love, a couple hunger and thirst ever more profoundly for the fullness of God and for the perfection of all creation in God.

Whatever the intensity of a couple's mutual love, knowing absolutely everything about each other is not essential for intimacy. Some specific knowledge indeed facilitates communication. However, there comes a point at which the couple have to transcend this form of insight. In going beyond specific knowledge about the other, each encounters the other's personhood at a depth not otherwise possible:

> By true love, and *a fortiori* by being-in-love,
> I know you in yourself,
> and not just something about you.

Paradoxically, in letting go the desire for specific knowledge about each other, the couple discover themselves united at unimaginable and inexpressible depths of intimacy. In that union, each receives a general, loving intuition of the other which transcends particular knowledge or concepts.

From one couple to another—whether considering marriage or already married—the intensity of mutual love varies. A

[1]See *O Blessed Night,* 63–67.

[2]See ibid., 57–68; *Receptivity,* 23-31.

couple may truly love one another, but neither may be in-love with the other or with anyone else. A couple may truly love each other and yet one partner experiences being-in-love with someone else. A couple may find that one person is in-love with the other, while the other simply loves him/her. Both the man and the woman may be mutually in-love. Yet, if God is calling a couple to matrimony, God will at least cause each to truly love the other and gift each with a need to enter into a lifelong conjugal relationship with the other.

Merely liking each other or only caring for one another does not suffice for an authentic vocation to married life. It is not enough that a couple are congenial, compatible or even close friends. All those qualities are carried forward to a new threshold when the couple truly love each other and even more so when they are in-love.

According to the canonical understanding of matrimony, God can call two persons to an authentic married life outside the sacrament: for example, two non-Christians. However, God does not call two persons to marriage—whether in the sacrament or outside it, as understood canonically—without gifting each with love for the other. So essential is true love that, if it is lacking, the couple may be united in some sense, but not in a way that is inseparable (Matt 19:6).

C. Pertinent Questions for Prospective Spouses

In evaluating the quality of their love then, two persons discerning a possible calling to marriage need to explore the following sets of questions:

> 1) What do I mean when I say "I love you"? Is my notion of love grounded in truth? Or is it founded on addiction, codependency or romantic idealism? Do I experience love principally as a spiritual quality? Or is it based primarily on physical or emotional attraction? Is there indication that this love will grow deeper as time passes? Do I long to grow old with this person?
>
> 2) Do I appreciate and respect the mystery of my intended spouse's personhood? What is my attitude towards his/her more mysterious depths? Am I threatened

by or fearful of his/her individuality? Do I remain in a basic stance of receptivity and awe as the mystery of the other gradually unfolds? Or am I trying to control my prospective spouse by demanding to know him/her through and through? Am I at home not knowing? Am I content to peacefully abide in the mystery of my intended partner?

3) What kind of affection am I experiencing? Do I at least truly love my prospective spouse? Do I love him/her dearly, tenderly? Am I in-love with my intended partner? Moreover, is my love such that it is urging me to spend the rest of my life in conjugal union with this person?

4) Do I have a sense of vocation about this marriage? Do I believe that God is calling us together to be the principal instruments of transformation and purification in each other's personal salvation history?

D. Countersigns of Authentic Love

A couple will want to examine whether or not they are mistaking infatuation, immature need or possessiveness for true love.

1) *Infatuation*

Infatuation connotes the exhilarating surge of being swept off one's feet. It suggests a certain folly or extravagance in admiration of another. Infatuation is like an emotional roller coaster. Falling in and out of love is a common sign of this experience. Infatuation is typical of adolescent affection.

Couples contemplating marriage will want to ask: Are strong feelings or physical attraction clouding my judgment? Am I so dazzled by the other that I am blind to reality? Am I in love with the idea of loving rather than experiencing true love for this person? Is what I call love little more than lust or self-centered gratification?

Basing a relationship, and *a fortiori* a marriage, on infatuation is like building a house on sand: "The rains came, the floods rose, the gales blew. They battered the house until it fell. And what a fall it had!" (Matt 7:27). If infatuation is the prime impulse, once the glitter fades and the emotions fizzle, no foundation remains for lasting commitment.

How do we distinguish infatuation from true love? Generally, the twofold test of time and familiarity prove the point. Since infatuation is so superficial, it can last only for a while. Familiarity, when there is no true love, breeds over time a certain contempt. Real lovers yearn to remain intimate, even after a certain familiarity sets in. In fact, the more they are together, the more they relish staying together.

We sometimes encounter situations that appear betwixt and between infatuation and love. There is a little depth, but nothing really lasting. There exists some sincerity mixed with much immaturity. Occasionally, the two persons enjoy romantic interludes or long for physical intimacies, but they unnerve each other if they have to be together too long, too frequently. Usually, this form of attraction is based more on need than on gift of self, as if to say:

> I need you,
> therefore, I "love" you more or less, once in a while.

Rather than:

> I love you,
> therefore, I need you more and more, all the time.

2) *Immature Need*

A need, generally speaking, is the absence of something which affects one's well-being. That well-being can refer to any of the dimensions of personhood: physical, sexual, affective, emotional, psychological, intellectual, spiritual.

If the absence pertains to something truly essential, we use words like "necessary," "indispensable," "requisite." To persist in this type of need is to experience privation; that is, the inability to attain well-being. If the absence pertains to something merely useful, we use terms like "missing," "wanting," "lacking." To persist in this kind of need is to experience inconvenience, but not deprivation in the strict sense.

Each person has genuine needs which must be met for health and wholeness. Most people possess also a host of needs, the fulfillment of which is not essential for happiness.

Frequently, these wants persist in the form of unconscious compulsions, drives or urges. Undue influence by immature desires or unmet developmental needs can negatively affect the choice of a spouse. Thus, the couple discerning a marital vocation have to ponder these questions:

Am I latching on to this person for any of the following reasons: a desire to escape parental domination; a craving for intimacy; a longing to have children; a way to quell feelings of loneliness; a yearning to rescue someone; a need to be needed?

Am I rushing into this relationship on the rebound? Am I desperate to marry? Do I view this opportunity as possibly my last chance for matrimony?

Is this prospective marriage appealing to me primarily because the other person can offer me power, wealth, security or social status?

3) *Possessiveness*

Possessiveness refers to a tendency of one person to control or to claim ownership of another. It indicates a lack of respect for the other's freedom and uniqueness. Frequently, possessiveness is encountered in persons suffering from codependency or excessive jealousy. The following questions ought to be examined by a couple considering marriage:

Do I view the other as a possession to attain, a conquest to make? Does the other person act toward me in an unduly demanding way? Are we turning in upon ourselves, trying to create a closed world for two?

Possessiveness may be indicated in the following types of behavior: very little or no socializing on the couple's part; frequent outbursts of jealousy; unremitting suspicion or mistrust concerning the other's fidelity or intentions; refusal to give the other the freedom to maintain healthy friendships; intolerance of the other's religious practices or convictions.

A couple must take care that they are not forming a symbiosis in which one tries to possess, while the other seeks to be dominated. A woman, for example, who is insecure or who desires to remain submissive may actually be flattered by a man's jealousy or by his insistence that she sever contact with others in order to be at his disposal. This dependent person may immaturely relinquish independence and freedom in lieu of feeling loved, wanted or useful.

Given the human condition, some infatuation, some immature need and a certain possessiveness ordinarily coexist with true love. It is then a question of degree. Love between a couple is imperfect at the outset. Only gradually does the Lord perfect and purify a covenant, thereby bringing the two persons into ever deeper union with one another in God. In terms of discernment, couples considering marriage, together with their spiritual guides, seek indication of an affective maturity sufficient to outweigh persisting immaturities.

CHAPTER 8

Mutual Conjugal Love

True love between a couple is integral to an authentic calling to matrimony. Whether that love progresses to loving tenderly and ultimately to being-in-love may depend as much on the husband's and the wife's ability to love as on God's gift of those intensifications to the couple. Some people are so wounded by trauma, abuse, abandonment, shame, codependency, etc. that their dysfunctionality[1] prevents them from reaching those depths of love this side of the resurrection.

Yet, loving one another or even being-in-love with each other does not of itself suffice for a vocation to marriage. It is possible for two persons to truly love one another without being called by God to a conjugal expression of that love. It is even possible that two people be-in-love with each other and not have a vocation to marry. Such could be the case between two individuals who are married but not to each other, between two celibates or between a single person and someone married or celibate. Thus, when there exists a vocation to wedded life, a complementary element qualifies the couple's love. It is mutually conjugal. That is, not only do the two persons truly love one another, but also they experience a calling to live out that love in a lifelong spousal relationship.

A. Two Characteristics of Conjugal Love

The conjugal dimension of loving, which is unique to a calling to marriage, is as difficult to define as love itself. Yet, its presence in a man and a woman called to wed each other ex-

[1]See *O Blessed Night*, 3–35.

hibits at least two characteristics: The couple need to share life together, and that shared life is all-embracing.

1) *A Need to Share Life Together*

A man and a woman called to marriage are interiorly impelled to commit themselves to each other for life. This need arises out of the inner dynamics of their mutual love as well as from a sense of vocation. As a consequence of the manner in which they love or are in-love, they yearn to express their affection in a covenanted way of life. Their longing is irresistible. In effect, each partner says to him/herself: "I cannot become me without a steady diet of you."

That need to share life together postulates equal partnership in every aspect of the marriage. The couple's union does not imply domination of one over the other. On the contrary, the New Testament advises all Christians, not only spouses:

> Be submissive to one another
> out of reverence for Christ (Eph 5:21).

"Be submissive" in this context does not mean capitulate, comply or conform; much less cower, abase oneself or grovel. It rather suggests acquiescence, respect, malleability—approaching one another in meekness, humility and gentleness. Applied to matrimony, that instruction in the Letter to the Ephesians accentuates *mutual* self-surrender, coequality and reciprocity within the complementarity of male and female. A marriage in which a couple fawn upon each other could indicate dysfunction in the relationship. A conjugal bond in which one spouse has to be subservient to the other does violence to the union. Whether subservience is of mind, will or body; whether it is psychological, emotional or physical, it is dehumanizing and ultimately destructive of mutual love, respect and submissiveness out of reverence for Christ.

Throughout history, each society has had its own role models for men and women. The author of Ephesians, for example, applies the above directive to the mores of his times (see Eph 5:22-33). Attitudes toward the interrelationship of the two sexes in marriage have progressed considerably in the twentieth century. Nonetheless, much more development is needed.

2) *Married Life as All-Embracing*

All-embraciveness is a second characteristic of conjugal love. A couple called to marriage view life together as the primary basis from which they daily live out their love for each other, for God and for creation. They realize that their marital relationship will influence every aspect of their existence. They desire to approach their involvement in the world uniquely as a married couple. Their experience runs something like this:

> I need you in order to become myself.
> Moreover, together we have to become ourselves in a relationship so intimate that it will determine our mode of living and of relating to others for the remainder of our lives.

The presence of those two characteristics in the experience of mutual love contributes an essential quality to the couple's readiness to consecrate themselves to each other and to God in the sacrament of matrimony.

B. Counterindications

For some couples, love does not point to marriage. A certain completeness without the intended partner, persistent self-doubt and lingering doubt regarding the prospective spouse are some of the more common counterindications of a calling to wedded life.

1) *A Certain Completeness Without One's Partner*

There is a sense in which every relatively mature individual—whether married, single or celibate—is complete. There is also a sense in which each person has to be complemented by another. We all need some solitude, and we all need some interaction.

A calling to marriage, however, postulates a certain *vocational* incompleteness without one's intended partner. That experience is integral to the couple's existential inability to become other than married together. The inverse is also an important principle of discernment: namely, to experience vocational completeness without any partner at all, or without a particular partner, constitutes a significant sign that God may not be calling one to marriage, or at least not to marriage with the person in question.

Sometimes that "completeness without" expresses itself in the form of an ennui—a wearisomeness, annoyance, tedium, boredom—with the other. A woman, for example, does not experience sufficient challenge in the relationship. A man, for instance, finds his fiancée's every thought, reaction, movement too predictable. There is no sense of the mystery and the bondedness which usually prevail when two people are called to live out their lives together in conjugal love. The spark is missing. The chemistry is simply not there.

Yet, that ennui differs radically from the aridity and emptiness which occur as love becomes more spiritualized.[2] When a vocation to marriage exists, each partner will inevitably experience in regard to the other some emptiness or lack of fulfillment. However, a sense of calling and an awareness of the transcendent depths of the loved one's personhood overshadow those factors. Ennui tends to deaden and to repel. Aridity arising from a maturing love is sobering and invites greater commitment.

In the case of vocations to celibacy or singlehood, that vocational completeness-without-another relates often to a need for solitude or for independence.

2) *Persistent Self-Doubt*

By the phrase "self-doubt," we mean that a prospective spouse begins to wonder if s/he is indeed called to the marriage in question. Self-doubt manifests itself in a variety of ways.

Despite the fact that a man is considering marriage with a woman whom he truly loves, he feels nonetheless a lack of intuitive thrust toward matrimony. For example, he goes to a friend's wedding. The ceremony is beautiful; the occasion is filled with joy and promise. Yet, as he witnesses the marriage, he cannot imagine himself standing there in the future and exchanging vows with his companion. He feels that he would be unable to go through with it. As a consequence of that realization, the man may confront his self-doubt and

[2]See *Spiritual Journey*, 102–113, 167–198.

thereby recognize that a call to marriage is questionable, or he may foolhardily try to deny that there is a problem.

Sometimes, a self-doubting person manages to make a verbal promise to marry. Yet, the fact that in practice s/he keeps deferring the formal engagement or cannot actually set a date for the nuptials reveals deep-seated hesitation.

The disinclination to marry one's prospective spouse may be camouflaged with a continuing stream of apparently legitimate excuses. For example, a woman claims that she wants to obtain a degree in nursing before embarking on marriage. Then after graduation, she insists on working for a while. That accomplished, she decides to go on for further studies before marriage. Having attained an advanced degree, she again defers the nuptials in order to work professionally. Her interest and study in health care could pertain to an authentic mission in life. However, she uses them to evade the fact that she has no real desire to marry her fiancé.

Assuming that her prospective spouse waits, the pattern of deferring commitment creates eventually an uneasy long-term relationship. Sooner or later, family and friends begin exerting pressure to move the hesitant woman to take a decisive step. That pressure further complicates an already precarious situation. After stringing her fiancé along for so long, she may find herself plagued with guilt. As tension mounts, she feels more and more trapped. Going ahead with the wedding may seem the only honorable way out of the dilemma. If she does so, the marriage will most likely fail.

Self-doubt reveals itself also in a certain form of unsettledness. A man, for example, has a sense that he will not find personal fulfillment in marriage with his fiancée. This type of restlessness differs radically from the inability to be satisfied[3] which every adult Christian experiences even after the discovery of one's vocation. Unsettledness can lead the man in a variety of nonproductive directions. He may, for instance, attempt to fill his inner void by frantic socializing or by promiscuous behavior. He may go the route of drugs, excessive eating or overindulgence in alcohol. He may secretively date someone other than his fiancée.

[3]See *Contemplation,* 62–65; *O Blessed Night,* 47–68; *Receptivity,* 18–31.

In some cases, people experience doubt about marrying because of a persistent attraction to another lifestyle. A woman, for example, may be drawn to commit herself as a celibate or to dedicate her life in the service of a cause which for her precludes marriage.

Prior to making a marital commitment, a man and a woman need to address all doubts about their desire for marriage in general and about each other in particular. Lingering doubts regarding an intended partner can indicate that marriage with him/her is inadvisable. Yet, there may still exist a calling to marry another person someday. Certain self-doubts arise from immaturities or dysfunctions. For the sake of continued growth, the person must resolve those deficiencies, whatever the final decision about marriage.

3) *Persistent Doubt about One's Prospective Spouse*

Disquieting behavior on the part of an intended spouse, especially when displayed repeatedly, can indicate lack of sufficient readiness to sustain married life. At the very least, these behavioral patterns indicate that marriage should be delayed until the would-be partner reaches greater maturity. Here are some examples:

A woman comes to see that her fiancé is very selfish. He expects her to make all the sacrifices, while he secures his own comfort and convenience.

A man finds that his intended wife frequently uses other people for personal gain. She has no real friends.

A woman becomes aware that her fiancé's parents and family still dominate him. He continues to conform to their expectations. He has not yet developed the independence and confidence necessary to be free from their dictates.

A man begins to suspect that his prospective wife lacks a sense of responsibility. She wastes money on nonessentials. She sees no need for sound budgeting and fiscal accountability. At work, she does only what is absolutely necessary to get by. There is a history of being unable to hold a job for very long.

A woman discovers that in a matter of importance her fiancé deliberately deceived her either by silence or by openly lying. She agonizes over his integrity, honesty and commitment.

A man has reason to doubt his fiancée's fidelity. Since they are not yet married, infidelity would not be conjugal in the strict sense. Nonetheless, the couple need to confront the matter.

A woman exhibits a pattern of subtle or outright indifference toward her future partner. She does not show him the degree of caring and tenderness that he has a right to expect.

The above signs—and others such as: heavy drinking, use of drugs, codependent behavior—give cause for concern and require thorough examination.

Mere absence of the above counterindications is not of itself a sign of a calling to marriage. To discern a vocation to matrimony, there must be positive indication of a love which impels the couple to covenant themselves to each other in an all-embracing lifestyle. In other words, to proceed with marriage, the couple needs to share a mutual conjugal love.

CHAPTER 9

Personal Maturity: Toward Peace in Conjugal Living

Jesus bequeaths his own peace to each of his disciples (John 14:27). Moreover, he invites every Christian to be a peacemaker (Matt 5:9). And in a specific way

> God has called [husbands and wives]
> to live in peace (1 Cor 7:15).

Being at home with oneself and being at home with the personality of one's spouse are prerequisite for peace in conjugal life. It takes considerable maturity to persevere in a marital relationship. Overall maturity can exist in a couple who do not have a vocation to marry each other. However, when God gifts a man and a woman with a calling to marriage, basic personal maturity is necessary for their conscious and free response to that vocation. Personal maturity is thus an important principle for discerning the authenticity of a possible calling to marriage.

In evaluating their personal maturity, a couple need to give attention to their respective life histories. Each prospective spouse can reflect on the following questions: How has the history of my life unfolded thus far? How do I see myself in the future? Am I ready to enter a permanent commitment with my intended partner? Have I reached the social, emotional, mental, psychological, sexual and spiritual maturity necessary for assuming and fulfilling the responsibilities of a marital covenant? Are my deficiencies or those of my future partner likely to handicap our conjugal relationship or to doom our marriage to failure?

In reviewing their life stories, the following specific areas merit careful attention: self-identity, self-knowledge, mutual insight, sexual orientation.

A. Self-Identity

The ability to make a Christian marital commitment presupposes that the man and the woman have each developed a strong and vigorous self for Christ.[1] In other words, the capacity to sustain a marital covenant presupposes that each possesses a basic individual identity.

Self-identity implies that a man or a woman has a sense of personal uniqueness. People who have established their identities appreciate the mystery of themselves and of others. They are in touch with their feelings and can express them appropriately. They stand in relation to others, yet see themselves as distinct from them. They are self-giving, yet can establish appropriate boundaries. They do not equate themselves with their friends, their relationships or their activities. While all those influences retain their relevance, mature persons are aware that they have a valid identity apart from them.

Self-identity implies also the ability to be self-determining. People with a sense of who they are do not live according to others' expectations. While they respect differing convictions and opinions, they assume responsibility for their own lives. They exercise the prudence and good judgment necessary to make their own choices and decisions, even at the risk of occasionally making a mistake or displeasing significant others.

Persons possessing sufficient self-identity usually have definite goals. These are not arbitrarily chosen, but rather have emerged after prolonged searching and experimentation with many options. These individuals have a sense of purpose in life. They are not drifting aimlessly, but are conscious of heading somewhere, even if the precise destination and the road thereto remain shrouded in mystery.

Individuals with a sense of self-identity are secure and confident. They are open to change. They are willing to modify

[1]See *Contemplation*, 116–121; *O Blessed Night*, 132–137; *Receptivity*, 83–88; *Spiritual Journey*, 55–74.

their perceptions and opinions in the light of new experiences or deeper knowledge.

Why is self-identity so important for a person discerning a possible vocation to matrimony? The reasons are primarily two: 1) Marriage is a mutual loving surrender between two people in the context of a shared life. Two "I's" become a "we" in such a way that each retains and grows in personal uniqueness. Yet, I cannot surrender myself to another until I first have a self to offer. Unless I possess a self, the other will possess me. In this case, two "I's" become a "me" as one person is absorbed in the other. That dynamic constitutes "submission" not in the evangelical sense of mutual respect and gentleness (Eph 5:21-22), but in a cowering or codependent sense. 2) A person who does not have a sufficient awareness of his/her identity lacks the inner freedom and maturity necessary for lifelong commitment.

Without a basic sense of self-identity in both the man and the woman, formidable difficulties are bound to occur. Suppose, for example, a wife tries to assume her husband's identity. Blindly, she pursues his goals and ambitions. His successes become her successes, and any failure on his part becomes her personal failure. As she fuses with him, she crowds him, impinges on his freedom and growth. He experiences the need to move further and further away from her stifling clutches. When separation or death removes him from her life, she is left agonizingly lost, without a personal identity of her own.

Lack of basic self-identity in one or both prospective partners is counterindicative of a calling to marriage. Three options face a couple when this deficiency is present: 1) They can terminate their relationship. 2) They can continue dating each other as well as others. 3) They can date exclusively, but without a commitment to marry. Since absence of self-identity is a fundamental human problem affecting every aspect of life, psychological counseling is advisable in all three options. If the couple pursue the second or the third course, the direction of their relationship needs continued discernment as each one changes.

Even when a man and a woman have attained basic self-identity, they are unlikely to be at the same point in personal maturity. Each one's growth proceeds at its own unique pace. Nonetheless, one greatly influences the other due to the all-embracing relationship which is developing between them.

B. Sufficient Knowledge

In this life love follows cognition, at least initially. That is, before I can love someone, I have to know that person. In the context of maturity between married partners, this truth has three immediate implications: 1) I cannot love another maturely until I love myself correctly. But, I cannot love myself correctly until I know myself sufficiently. 2) I cannot love another truly until I also know him/her adequately. Without that knowledge, I would be loving my image of the other and not the real person. 3) I cannot love either myself or another in the sense of *agápe* until I know both myself and the other as loved unconditionally by God. Therefore, a man and a woman considering marriage need to discern the quality of their self-knowledge and of their knowledge of each other.

Once a couple do love, however, that love transcends their knowledge of self or of each other and pursues its own course of intensity. Furthermore, love provides an intuitive knowledge all its own. This intuitive knowledge is commonly called "wisdom." It flows from the couple's direct experience of one another in love. This knowledge of the heart—which reason cannot know—does not consist in specific concepts or thoughts. Nor is it made up primarily of precise details about the beloved. It attests:

> I know you more deeply
> because I love you,

rather than:

> I love you
> because I know so much about you.

In this section we do not focus on the question of loving knowledge. Instead, we concentrate on the specific knowledge of self and of the other which is necessary for harmonious conjugal living. That knowledge flows from a sense of self-identity.

1) *Self-Knowledge*

The man and the woman discerning a call to marriage need to ponder the following questions related to their experience of themselves:

Have I come to a fundamental grasp of who I am, where I am going, what I want in life? Or am I still trying to find myself? Regardless of chronological age, am I still wondering what I want to be when I grow up?

How well do I know myself: my temperament, my dominant characteristics? In the process of maturation, have I been able to recognize my God-given talents and potential? What are my special gifts? To what degree have I developed or squandered them? Is the positive aspect of my self-image balanced with a realistic awareness of my limitations, weaknesses and sinfulness?

Do I accept myself as I am? Do I maintain a healthy self-love in the actual experience of the positive and negative dimensions of my personality?

Am I patient and gentle with myself in my stumbling and falling? Or am I harsh and condemning? Persons who cannot accept themselves in their own weaknesses are unlikely to be compassionate toward their spouses in theirs.

How do I deal with hurt, anger, disappointment, failure—all of which occur from time to time in any marital relationship? Do I pout, give the silent treatment, throw temper tantrums or become violent? A basic inability to deal constructively with negative feelings related to one's intended spouse or his/her family of origin is indicative of unreadiness for marriage. Furthermore, a person may need professional help to work through those immaturities.

Am I forgiving? Or do I harbor resentment, hold grudges, never let another forget an offense? In such an intimate relationship as marriage, where each person is so vulnerable, spouses have to be ready to forgive over and over again.

2) *Mutual Knowledge*

Besides self-knowledge a man and a woman considering marriage need a thorough understanding of one another. A lover spontaneously yearns to know the beloved more. That knowledge is primarily knowing the person in his/her mysterious self. It entails also knowing as much as possible about the beloved. To know the beloved and to know about the beloved require attentive listening and effective communication.

How well do I know the person whom I want to marry? Have I listened to my prospective spouse in order to discover his/her values, interests, concerns, goals and expectations? Am I aware of his/her usual defense mechanisms? Do I love this person in his/her inner poverty? Am I empathetic and compassionate when confronted with his/her immaturities?

Even though in marriage two become one, neither spouse surrenders individuality. Therefore, a certain privacy is always appropriate. My spouse, for example, is not my confessor, therapist or spiritual director. Nonetheless, a basic openness must persist in all areas, even sensitive ones. Thus, am I willing to let myself be known by my prospective spouse? Can I honestly reveal my thoughts, feelings, fears, strengths and weaknesses? Or do I need to put up a front, to wear a mask suitable for each occasion, to shut out the other from my private world?

How well does my future partner know me? Is my intended spouse willing to accept me as I am? Or does this person refuse to see anything which contradicts his/her fantasy of me? Do I perceive the other as having an idealistic picture of me? Is my prospective spouse in love with an image of me which s/he has concocted?

Encounters in many diverse situations over a prolonged time are the natural milieus in which the couple develop specific knowledge of each other. Over many months—preferably several years—they must give themselves leisure to experience one another. They need to be alone together, to socialize with their respective friends, to get to know their future in-laws, to become acquainted with each other's work environment, to worship God together. Through all these means the couple acquire a realistic knowledge of themselves and of their relationship.

The quality of the couple's specific knowledge of each other converges then on three points:

a) Each partner can identify his/her own real desires and needs, as well as those of the other.

b) Each one has the ability to respond meaningfully to the other's legitimate desires and needs.

c) Each one remains willing, if not eager, to address the other's legitimate desires and needs.

Without knowledge of one another's most cherished aspirations, together with ability and willingness to interact at those levels, in-depth communion between a man and a woman is impossible.

3) *Three Particularly Delicate Issues*

The closeness of the marital bond and the intimacy of conjugal life require that a couple confront—before the wedding—the following delicate issues:

a) Does there exist in my intended spouse's family of origin any form of chemical dependency, such as drugs or alcohol? Also, is there evidence of wife, husband or child abuse, whether sexual, emotional or physical? Children of chemically dependent parents and victims of abuse come from dysfunctional family systems. Unless they identify and become free from those patterns of interaction, these persons tend to repeat them.[2]

b) Independent of my proposed spouse's family, does s/he exhibit any signs of chemical dependency or drug-related problems—past, present or likely in the future?

c) Independent of my intended partner's family background, does s/he give indication of future spouse or child abuse—whether that potential be sexual, emotional or physical?

Before making a lifelong commitment, a person must resolve with the intended spouse any suspicion—let alone evidence—that one of the above situations exists. Open discussion of the problem—whether actual or potential—is a first step in the right direction. A second step is mutual agreement on a course of action should such a difficulty surface in the future. Since tendencies toward abuse are often latent, psychological and personality testing with mutual comparison and discussion of results is also advisable.

[2]See *O Blessed Night,* 1–44.

Problems of addiction and family abuse are often of a compulsive nature. Thus, love and goodwill alone do not suffice for recovery. In most situations, all persons affected—even those not specifically addicted—require psychological counseling.

C. Sexual Orientation and Compatibility

Sexual intercourse is ordinarily an essential dimension of the conjugal relationship. Thus, prior to marriage a man and a woman have to discern carefully the quality of their sexual maturity. Moreover, within the scope of their engagement, they need to discover whether or not they are sexually compatible.

A pattern of recurrent homosexual or bisexual involvements on the part of a person contemplating marriage frequently indicates ambiguity regarding psychosexual identity and sexual preference. Resolution of that ambiguity is necessary before the person enters a conjugal relationship. When the individual experiencing sexual ambiguity is already married, s/he needs to resolve the question of sexual orientation before making a decision about the future of the existing bond.

In the case of sexual ambiguity, the following questions need to be confronted:

Am I basically homosexual, heterosexual or bisexual? Have homosexual desires or involvements arisen primarily from curiosity or need for affection? Or are they symptomatic of a fundamental homosexual bent which precludes the type of heterosexual exchange which my partner has a right to expect in marriage? Resolution of those questions usually demands much time and honest searching, as well as competent assistance.

Am I inclined toward any form of sexual addiction: fetishism, transvestism, zoophilia, pedophilia, exhibitionism, voyeurism, sexual masochism, sexual sadism, etc.? Tendencies toward, and *a fortiori* acting out, any of the paraphilias require psychological evaluation. Their presence can, in fact, indicate an incapacity for marriage.

Many sincere Christians experience a definite homosexual

orientation. Yet, because of a climate of condemnation, widespread homophobia and their own personal anxieties, some of those people try to deny or to repress their true sexual identity. In desperation, a few of them mistakenly think that marriage offers an answer to their predicament. They naively assume that by entering a marital relationship, their sexual orientation might eventually turn heterosexual or at least appear socially acceptable. They hope that in marriage the struggles associated with their homosexuality will pass or remain covered up. That is misguided reasoning. Any nuptial entered into with those unrealistic expectations is bound to fail. Forging ahead with the marriage would indeed be unjust to one's partner and to oneself. Moreover, the nuptial bond would probably be invalid.

A bisexual orientation poses a very difficult problem in discerning a possible vocation to marriage. The bisexual partner would have to be up front with his/her mate regarding the twofold direction of the sexual orientation. Furthermore, the bisexual partner would need to show convincing signs of an ability to remain faithful for life to one person of the opposite sex and to find personal fulfillment in the intended marriage.

When heterosexual orientation is present, both partners still have to consider the quality of their sexual maturity. Have the man and the woman passed successfully through the preadolescent and adolescent phases of psychosexual development? If not, they are ill-prepared for marriage. Have they been able to practice a form of chastity which accords with their engaged status? Persons with low sexual impulse control will not likely find the inner resources required for fidelity after marriage or for abstinence from sexual intercourse when necessary in marriage.

Furthermore, how do the couple view sexual intercourse itself? Is it an act of love, or is it nothing more than physical satisfaction? Do they perceive sexual intercourse as an expression of mutual loving surrender which encompasses their whole being in its physical, psychological and spiritual dimensions? Or do they see sexual intercourse in marriage as merely the legitimization of sexual activity? Do they look upon it as the prime reason for togetherness in a conjugal relationship? Do the couple's attitudes harmonize regarding the place of sexual intercourse within the marriage, or do irreconcilable differences persist?

Finally, what about the couple's desire for sexual intercourse and their actual expressions of love? Are these characterized by a compulsiveness which seeks self-gratification and shows little or no concern for the other? Or is each partner able to respect the rhythm of the other's response in romantic interchange?

Thus, signs of personal maturity on the part of a person considering a possible vocation to marriage include: the presence of a basic self-identity, sufficient self-knowledge, realistic insight into the intended spouse and clarity regarding sexual preference. Personal maturity facilitates a Christian's ability to live a conjugal life in the peace of Christ—a peace which the world cannot give or take away (John 14:27).

CHAPTER 10

Harmonious Interaction: Toward Deeper Peace in Marriage

Along with personal maturity, harmonious interaction between a couple contributes greatly to their ability to live their conjugal life in the peace of Christ (1 Cor 7:15; John 14:27).

The quality of the couple's interaction is thus another important principle in discerning a possible calling to marriage. In the previous chapter, we saw how personal maturity forms a necessary substratum for a couple's interaction. In this chapter, we examine four factors which influence the positive development of that interaction: interdependence, complementarity, solitude and spirituality.

A. Interdependence

Spouses are mutually dependent for much of their psychological, emotional and spiritual growth. That interdependence lies at the heart of their vocational need for each other.

Interdependence means considerably more than team effort and mutual cooperation. The ability to participate in joint activities contributes to a vibrant marital relationship. Collaborative endeavors offer opportunities for developing communication skills, for transcending individualism and for respecting the interests of the other. Success in those areas gives positive indication that a person can assume the self-giving and the self-sacrificing which are so essential in wedded life. However, the interdependence whereof we speak is essentially vocational, because God is its source, its goal and its sustaining force. This interdependence is directly related to the couple's ability to become fully themselves in the Lord.

No one person or group of people can fulfill all the needs of another human being. Whether married or unmarried, everyone experiences unmet spiritual, emotional, psychological, sexual and physical wants. God does not intend that all our needs be completely met this side of the resurrection. Nonetheless, there are specific needs which by divine calling one's spouse alone can satisfy. These needs relate to the salvation histories of the two spouses. That is, the Lord wills that until death parts them this husband and wife be the principal instruments within each other's lives of God's transforming and purifying activity. Because this instrumentality occurs primarily within the nitty-gritty of daily existence, facets of it are discernible. Yet, since it is God forming one through the other, this instrumentality remains mysterious and often not readily apparent.

The God-intended interdependence of marriage does not jeopardize the individual identity of either spouse. On the contrary, the interdependence of the husband and the wife facilitates both their personal and collective maturation. The mutual calling to matrimony enhances the uniqueness of each partner. The more the two "I's" mature as a "we," the more each "I" burgeons as an individual, though vocationally interdependent, person. By the same token, as each spouse develops, the couple grow in oneness.

Examples of immature dependence of one spouse on the other abound. Yet, that fact does not negate the proper role of mature interdependence in the conjugal relationship. Therefore, crucial questions for persons discerning a possible vocation to wedded life are these:

> Do we need one another mainly because we love each other and believe that God is calling us to marriage?
> Or are we attracted to one another primarily because we need each other (or at least, because I need you)?

The first is healthy and invigorating interdependence. The second is immature dependency and possibly not true love at all.

B. Complementarity

Complementarity between a man and a woman enhances harmonious interaction.

1) Complementarity can result when two opposite characteristics are held in creative tension. Consider these examples: One person is meticulous. The other is disorganized. However, each affects the other with the result that both become more moderate. One person is nervous, high-strung and talkative. The other is calm, quiet and reserved. Yet, they influence each other's personalities so that both develop more evenly.

In terms of Jungian personality types, complementarity can readily exist between an *extrovert* and an *introvert,* a *sensate* and an *intuitive* individual, a *judging* and a *perceiving* person. Understandably, those correlations do not exist without some tension and occasional misinterpretation. However, when the couple are opposites on the *thinking* and the *feeling* modes of processing experience, that combination frequently causes each spouse considerable anxiety. The predominately thinking partner often misunderstands the particulars of the feeling spouse's need for affection. Rarely is the thinking mate capable of satisfying the other's emotive demands. Moreover, the thinking person is often overwhelmed by barrages of emotion from his/her mate. The two may love each other with equal intensity, but they express their love differently. To achieve harmony, each partner has to learn to respect the differences in the other. The thinking person must make extra effort to express tenderness and affection. The feeling partner has to back off from excessive emotive demands and let go unrealistic expectations.

2) Complementarity can occur also when prospective spouses share a common interest or gift. Suppose, for example, that a couple are furnishing a home. Having similar tastes in interior decorating, they quickly agree on a basic plan. As they proceed, a creative change by one engenders a correspondingly creative arrangement by the other. Or take a couple who are professional colleagues working together on a research project. Because of a shared vision, each may be able to bring refinement and precision to the other's thought. Thus, they proceed together toward a greater comprehension of truth, one

from a mainly masculine perspective, the other from a primarily feminine point of view.

However, not all persons perceive their differences in a complementary manner. A couple may experience certain differences as irreconcilable. Consider a man and a woman with a wide gap between their levels of education. Suppose the woman is a college graduate, while the man is a high school dropout. This couple may find little or no intellectual meeting ground despite a genuine affection for each other. Furthermore, their respective educational backgrounds will influence their social relationships. The college graduate will probably have many friends with similar intellectual interests, whereas the high school dropout will gravitate toward people with virtually no academic inquisitiveness. The differences in values, interests and acceptable social behavior between the two circles of acquaintances may become impossible to bridge. Each may turn out to be an embarrassment to the other.

Another example: A man's value system is such that he is content with employment that earns the minimum wage. He is happy to live frugally and seeks no more than the bare necessities of life. He has no desire to acquire wealth, power or prestige. To his prospective wife, that outlook seems lazy and complacent, not to mention lacking in ambition and initiative. She herself is highly motivated and goal-oriented. She wants not only to improve herself, but also to mold her future husband into an image she has conceived for him. She thinks that when they marry she will be able to bring about that transformation. In reality, however, her endeavor will probably result in conflict and frustration. If they hold firmly to their respective outlooks, this couple will drift apart. The more the man refuses to change, the more the woman will seethe with resentment toward him.

Sharply differing or irreconcilable expectations of married life also reflect incompatibility between a couple. The following are two examples:

1) The woman desires to combine a career with marriage. She plans on having no more than two children. Moreover, she wants to delay beginning a family until she establishes herself professionally. The man, on the other hand, believes that his prospective wife should forego her career in order to be

a homemaker. He hopes for at least five children and yearns to begin a family immediately. Unless this couple can reach an agreement which carries with it inner peace for both, marriage is inadvisable.

2) The intended wife sees marriage and family as central in her life. The future husband's first priority is single-minded dedication to his career. Should a marriage result in this instance, the wife and children will probably experience a great deal of neglect and frustration.

Just as differences can be antagonistic rather than complementary, so too similarities. A couple who share personality traits or interests which are too similar may end up bored with each other. Instead of stimulating one another to further growth, each has to look elsewhere for challenge and diversion.

Even when a man and a woman experience themselves as generally complementary, certain areas of tension and conflict are bound to persist. In those areas the two will have to make adjustments, modifications and compromises if they hope to live together in peace. For a married couple, that struggle is a crucial aspect of taking up their cross daily to follow Christ (Luke 9:23).

C. Solitude in Conjugal Life

Personal solitude is an inescapable dimension of human life. Everyone needs to be alone sometimes. Therefore, persons called to marriage have to consider also the solitary aspect of their conjugal vocation.

Some spiritual guides use the word "celibate" to designate this solitary element within married life. We believe, however, that "solitude/solitary" more accurately expresses the quality at issue. We prefer to reserve the term "celibate" for that Christian lifestyle which we treat next in this book.

The question arises: What is the relationship between solitude and harmonious interaction for a married couple? In a nutshell, knowing how to be alone and how to be distinctly oneself is necessary in order for the couple to be more deeply one.

Married people experience solitude in basically two ways: 1) as part of the process of individuation which each spouse undergoes and 2) as an aspect of each partner's personal relationship with God. In both respects, one spouse is the privileged instrument through which God brings the other to a deeper consciousness of solitude.

1) *The Individuation Process*

Through their love for one another expressed in Christian marriage, a man and a woman become one in Christ's love. That dialectic is a sign of God's love for them as well as for everyone (Matt 19:4-5; 1 Cor 6:16; Eph 5:31). So united by love are a couple that in Christ each abides in the other. That oneness in the Lord's own love constitutes the sacramental value of Christian matrimony. Both husband and wife celebrate their union of heart, soul, mind and body in a myriad of ways.

Yet, the union of a man and a woman in Christian marriage does not cause absorption of one person into the other. On the contrary, true union always differentiates. As the couple become more united in love, each becomes more his/her unique self. God intends that each spouse attain over the course of wedded life a certain measure of personal development. While the couple share many common values and interests, each has ordinarily some values and interests which the other does not completely embrace.

The process of individuation brings each married person to the following experience of selfhood: "I possess my unique individuality, my own life, my singular destiny. I am called to make a specific contribution to the life of my spouse as well as to the world." That experience of the mystery of one's developing personhood is the milieu for encounter with God as the loving giver of that self as well as for solidarity with others in God. This solitude and solidarity open the person ever deeper to the spiritual dimension of existence.

A couple considering a vocation to Christian marriage need to appreciate the solitary aspects of their respective processes of individuation. A person's ability to accept the other's uniqueness, together with his/her own, is a sign of readiness to enter a lifelong marital commitment. Because an individual is constantly growing, the capacity to accept ongoing change in an intended partner, as well as in the relationship itself, is a further necessary quality for marriage.

2) *Each Spouse's Relationship with God*

However deeply one may love the other and however meaningful their conjugal life remains, every married couple comes sooner or later to this paradoxical situation: Both persons experience a certain emptiness and a lack of fulfillment which their relationship cannot assuage.

Two factors converge to produce that experience. First, the spouse and married life itself are fulfilling their providential role. They are pointing the person beyond them to God. Second, the person is also being confronted with his/her inability to be totally satisfied by anyone or anything except God.[1] No human being—or succession of relationships—can ever completely quell the restlessness of the human heart. Ultimately, only Father, Son and Spirit can entirely satisfy its deepest longings and desires:

> You have made us for yourself, O Lord,
> and our heart is restless until it rests in you.[2]

Thus, conjugal love becomes instrumental in bringing each spouse to that depth of personhood where s/he remains alone with God. Paradoxically, that solitude is also a basis for shared intimacy. Abiding in loving communion with the Lord, each partner enters more deeply into loving union with the other and with all creation in God.

When the Spirit leads us into solitude of heart to commune with God, we experience the necessity for some exterior solitude as well. We need time and space to "remain loving our Beloved."[3] That truth applies to everyone, whether married, single or celibate. A married person naturally has to discern the amount of time advisable for exterior solitude in the light of all other aspects of conjugal life.

In discerning the solitary dimension of Christian marriage, each couple does well to ponder these questions:

Am I unrealistically expecting my intended partner to satisfy all the longings of my heart? Am I trying to use this relation-

[1]See *O Blessed Night*, 47–68; *Receptivity*, 17–31; *Contemplation*, 62–65.

[2]St. Augustine, *Confessions*, 1, 1 (*PL* 32:661; *CCSL*, 27:1).

[3]"*Estarse amando al Amado,*" St. John of the Cross, *Sum of Perfection*, 4. See *Contemplation*, 21–26, 36–43.

ship to fill a void which God alone can satisfy? Am I demanding from my prospective spouse what God alone can give?

Or do I peacefully accept my inability to be completely satisfied by anyone or anything but God? Do I joyfully and gratefully look upon my intended spouse as the most significant person whom the Lord will use to draw me closer to God?

Can I integrate into my marriage the interior and the exterior solitude to which God calls me? Can my prospective partner and I support each other in accepting and undergoing the Lord in solitude?

D. Certain Spiritual Issues

A Christian couple discerning a possible vocation to marriage will want to reflect on their interaction with regard to certain issues directly affecting their spiritual life.

1) *The Couple's Spirituality*

Every human being has a spirituality, because everyone has a capacity to experience God personally and to respond individually to the Lord. Each person has a unique way of relating with God.

Who is Jesus for each prospective spouse? What needs flow from each one's relationship with Christ?

Can the couple respect one another's inner promptings? For example, is the prospective wife willing to support her future husband in making an occasional retreat, serving on parish committees or being a daily communicant? Will the husband-to-be encourage his intended wife to take time for solitary prayer, for service on a parish council or for teaching catechetics? If one is inclined toward quiet meditation and the other toward charismatic prayer, can the couple peacefully accept their differences?

In terms of family prayer—such as the Rosary and Sunday worship—what are the expectations of each prospective spouse? Are their expectations compatible?

2) *Puritanical Attitudes Toward Sex*

Occasionally, one still finds prudish attitudes toward conjugal expressions of love. Some people have not only warped moral notions regarding sex, but also a veritable scrupulosity regarding sexual practices.

A spouse may believe that sexual intercourse is appropriate only for the procreation of children. Another imagines that it is intrinsically holier to abstain from lovemaking during Advent and Lent. Some men still worry about "spilling the seed," while some women want to keep their eyes closed and think of something pleasant until "it" is over.

People with distorted views on conjugal expressions of love need moral, spiritual and frequently psychological help. Their spouses also may benefit from seeking assistance to cope with their partner's puritanical attitudes and sexual scrupulosity.

3) *Dichotomies*

Some people separate love for Christ from love for their spouses, children and others. They think, and at times speak, in terms of who comes first, second and third in their affection. That attitude frequently causes feelings of alienation, rejection and jealousy in those closest to them.

In reality, the dichotomy is a pseudo-problem. It is not a question of choosing one love over another, but of integrating all one's loves with love for God. The Lord has called the married couple to become both one in themselves and one in God.

Some married persons struggle with another pseudo-problem: Which do I opt for—family or Church; my spouse and children or my parish? This issue becomes increasingly relevant as more lay people are drawn into full-time employment in ministerial positions. The real issue here is usually how much time, energy and effort is God inviting an individual to invest in each calling. Both family life and ministry are authentic forms of Christian mission. It is a matter of proper proportion, not of one over the other. Since spouse and family remain the basic vocational responsibility, that commitment must always receive a qualitative investment of time and energy. Undue tension does not stem from a dichotomy between family life and ministerial service in themselves. Rather, its source lies often in a distorted attitude toward those two integrable aspects of Christian vocation.

Couples considering marriage thus need to discern the following questions: Am I setting my love for my future spouse and my commitment to Christ in opposition to each other? Can I situate my love for my future husband or wife in the context of my relationship with Jesus? In pondering our conjugal life, do I foresee basic harmony between my family life and other ministerial involvements? Or do I envisage only excessive tension or irresolvable conflict between those two aspects of my spiritual journey?

Interdependence, complementarity, solitude, respect for each other's spirituality foster harmonious interaction between a husband and a wife. Moreover, these gifts are signs of the peace which a couple receive when they are one in Christ.

CHAPTER 11

Pastoral Applications

A relational model of marriage differs from the classical parental and behavioral models. According to these models, matrimony is viewed primarily in terms of procreation of children and secondarily in terms of mutual assistance and remedy for concupiscence. In a relational model, the focus is the love relationship of a husband and wife united in Christ by a specific calling from God. That love-covenant between the couple unfolds vis-á-vis one another, their children (if any), God and all creation. In a relational model, two spouses are seen as the principal instruments of God's transforming and purifying activity in each other's lives.

Although we have not dealt in detail with procreation of children as a principle of discernment for marriage, it is not that we consider establishing a family unimportant. Rather, we look upon parenting as a specific vocation in its own right—a mission to which God calls many married couples, but not necessarily all. Thus, parenting is a vocation with its own constellation of signs and conditions. Because the subject is so complex, we elect not to treat it here.

We conclude this section on principles for discerning a vocation to the conjugal life by offering a summary of the signs and conditions integral to that discernment. We offer also reflections on certain pastoral situations which arise in the process of evaluating possible callings to matrimony.

A. Options for Marriage: Decision in Faith

In a relational model of marriage, the signs and conditions for discernment include the following:

1) A man and a woman possess sufficient emotional, psychological, affective and sexual maturity.

2) Evident in their relationship are adequate self-understanding, knowledge of each other and sense of self-identity.

3) The couple experience interdependence; that is, mutual self-surrender, coequality and reciprocity within male-female complementarity.

4) They exhibit a sufficient degree of social, personal and sexual complementarity.

5) Each partner values personal solitude and privacy.

6) The couple possess compatible religious convictions and spiritual interests.

7) Their interaction gives indication that they will be able to share wedded life in evangelical peace and harmony.

8) The man and the woman truly love each other in such a way that the inner dynamics of that love impel them toward a conjugal covenant for the rest of their earthly sojourn.

9) The couple have a meaningful sense that God is calling them together in matrimony.

10) They experience an existential inability to become otherwise. That is, the man and the woman are conscious of a vocational imperative emanating from deep within them. They believe that in order to mature into the persons whom God is destining them to be, they have to do so as a married couple.

Those signs and conditions are to be understood as an ensemble. The last three taken together are the most crucial in discerning a marital vocation. The first seven by themselves do not give compelling indication of a vocation to matrimony. For instance, complementarity between a man and a woman or profound mutual caring does not necessarily mean that God is calling them to this sacrament. Yet, each of those seven principles remains integral to the overall discernment process. When all ten principles coexist—although in varying degrees—they converge to give convincing indication that God may indeed be calling a man and a woman to consecrate themselves in marriage to each other and to Christ.

Ultimately, however, the decision to marry is an option taken in faith:

- faith in God and in each other,
- faith tried in the crucible of time,
- faith attested by signs,
- faith seeking understanding,
- faith which remains dark and risk-filled yet impelling,
- faith that prompts the heart to recognize reasons that reason could never articulate.

The following words from the "instruction" of a time-honored marriage rite address the implications of that faith commitment:

> This union . . . will bind you together for life in a relationship so close and so intimate that it will profoundly influence your whole future. That future, with its hopes and disappointments, its successes and failures, its pleasures and pains, its joys and sorrows, is hidden from your eyes. You know that these elements are mingled in every life and are to be expected in your own. And so, not knowing what is before you, you take each other for better or for worse, for richer or for poorer, in sickness and in health, until death. Truly, then, these words are most serious. It is a beautiful tribute to your undoubted faith [in God and] in each other, that, recognizing their full import, you are nevertheless so willing and ready to pronounce them.[1]

B. Pastoral Situations

When most people begin contemplating marriage, they are single and are looking for an appropriate spouse. Thus, they are inclined toward conjugal life, but do not know yet with whom. Marriage understood as a divine calling may or may not have occurred to them. The fact that marriage entails the

[1] *Collectio Rituum* (New York: Benziger Bros., 1964) 290.

convergence of the callings of two people compounds the discernment process. Frequently, the couple are at different stages of vocational consciousness. Too often, one or both have no vocational awareness at all.

Persons involved in marriage preparation or in counseling those already married encounter a variety of pastoral situations. Here are a few of the more common:

First, in the context of marriage preparation:

1) Both prospective spouses so love each other that they experience the essence of what we have termed "an existential inability" to become other than married. Moreover, they want to celebrate that conjugal intimacy in a sacramental manner.

2) One of the engaged persons has attained mature vocational awareness, the other has not. Yet, there is reasonable hope that s/he will eventually do so. The couple insist on proceeding with the wedding, and trust that their love will sustain them.

3) Neither prospective spouse has reached mature vocational consciousness. Yet, they press on toward the wedding, willing to make the tough choices if their marriage does not work out.

4) The couple, although they desire an elaborate church wedding, have no inkling of marriage as a vocation. They have no meaningful sense of being called by God to share a lifelong covenant. They just want to get married and then see what develops.

5) The prospective spouses are willing to postpone the ecclesial celebration of their marriage until both have experienced mature vocational awareness.

Second, in the context of counseling persons already married:

1) Each had fallen in love with the other and had wanted to marry. There was little or no vocational consciousness at the time of the wedding. Years later they realize that, regardless of what God's will for them may have been in the past, the Lord is now calling them to

remain married for the rest of their life. Thus, both finally reach mature vocational awareness.

2) Even though no third-party is involved, one of the spouses has come to believe that there is no divine calling to remain in the present marriage. This is often the case when the couple entered matrimony out of projective identification.

3) A spouse has attained mature vocational awareness, only to realize that God seems to be calling him/her to marry someone else. What to do, especially when children are involved?

C. Pastoral Challenges

Within the context of a relational model, a number of pastoral challenges confront the discernment of a possible vocation to Christian marriage.

1) *The Responsibility of Spiritual Guides*

People with ministerial experience in premarital or marriage counseling have probably already made an observation like this: All those principles are right on target. Practically speaking, however, they require an enormous amount of time and energy to implement. Far too many couples are ill-prepared for matrimony. When most of them come for counseling, their minds are already so set that for them vocational discernment is not an issue. Many couples want only to dispense with the formalities as quickly as possible and to get on with the wedding.

There is much truth in the above observations. Nonetheless, as pastors, directors and counselors we must find a way to inculcate in would-be spouses an awareness of the principles for discernment, and we must guide couples in applying these principles to their situation. Until we exert every effort in that regard, we ourselves remain remiss in a significant aspect of our own calling. Many steps in the right direction have already been taken. Many long strides still need to follow.

This then is a first pastoral imperative: We really do have to find a way to impart a more profound vocational consciousness in prospective and already married persons. The truth and seriousness of the matter cry out for that effort.

2) *Marriage: A Vocation in Its Own Right*

Some Christians assume that if God does not call a person to celibacy, s/he is thereby destined to marry. That reasoning is flawed. Marriage is a vocation in its own right. It is not something left over after celibacy is ruled out.

By way of fostering an awareness of marriage as a unique calling, a twofold focus is helpful in catechesis: (a) a vocation to marriage in general and (b) a calling to marriage with a specific person.

3) *Adequate Readiness for Marriage*

Ideally, prospective spouses should decide upon a date for their wedding only after they have been courting each other for about a year. It takes considerable time, extensive effort and a diversity of circumstances to attain the knowledge necessary to make a sound lifelong commitment. Ordinarily, both would-be spouses ought to be at least in their twenties, have completed their undergraduate education and have embarked upon their respective careers, if indeed each intends to pursue one. The basic maturity required for a sacramental covenant predicates this care in discerning.

The need for well-designed personality tests to help couples know themselves cannot be overemphasized. However, it does not suffice merely to take a test and to receive the results. A competent evaluator has to explain in detail to the couple the implications of their respective typologies for their wedded life.

If a couple do not arrive at an explicit realization of a mutual existential inability to be other than married for life to one another, they are not yet ready to make a lifelong commitment. Therefore, a church wedding is inadvisable. In this case, the key sign which God alone can furnish is lacking. A couple must resolve any serious doubt regarding their mutual vocation prior to the celebration of the sacrament, no matter how long the process takes.

What can be done if the couple insist on marriage notwithstanding the lack of necessary vocational awareness? One possible solution would be for the Church to permit a civil marriage without ecclesial stigma. Then, when the couple attain sufficient vocational consciousness, they could have their union convalidated. This pastoral practice, however, would require change in the current Code of Canon Law.

What if the prospective husband and wife are not practicing their faith but ask to be married in a church? Most couples who do not practice their faith care little or not at all about marrying in the Church. A sense of marriage as a God-given vocation is virtually nonexistent in them. Yet, many of their parents, grandparents or significant others do care a great deal and exert enormous pressure on both the couple and the pastor. Admittedly, there are many angles to each situation. But, if pastors were permitted to encourage a civil marriage without ecclesial stigma, that option would enable them to address sensitively the intricacies at issue. It would eliminate the dilemma of outrightly denying the couple a church wedding or of proceeding with the formal nuptials as if there were no problem.

Implementation of that possible civil marriage option for couples not practicing their faith would require considerable change in present ecclesial legislation as well as reeducation of both clergy and laity. Theologically, this change seems viable. Moreover, for the spiritual good of certain couples it appears also desirable.

4) *Premarital Pregnancy*

A premarital pregnancy poses special problems regarding a possible vocation of the father and the mother to marriage.

A first scenario supposes that the pair were not seriously considering marriage to each other. If, however, they begin contemplating matrimony after learning of the pregnancy, then neither a civil nor a church wedding is advisable until after the the child's birth. Marriage should never be embarked upon primarily for reasons of convenience, duty or cover-up.

A second scenario supposes that the couple had been seriously considering marriage prior to the pregnancy. Perhaps they were already engaged. Even though many factors come into play, it is usually more prudent in this case to postpone the church wedding. The moral pressures resulting from the unexpected pregnancy are so formidable that neither the man nor the woman can continue a meaningful discernment until after the child is born and emotions have subsided. If the couple insist on marrying, one option could be for the Church to permit them a civil wedding without stigma. When the time is ripe, a convalidation could follow. According to current ecclesial law, however, pastors cannot recommend this civil marriage option.

Should the couple decide not to marry, they must carefully weigh the child's spiritual, psychological and physical well-being. Among their options are these three: a) Give the child up for adoption. b) Place the baby in temporary custody (e.g., with a relative), until the man and the woman discern their future. c) Either the mother or the father keep the child as a single parent.

5) *Married Couples Without an Authentic Vocation*

What happens in the case of two people already married who discern that they do not have a vocation to share conjugal life with one another? In these painful situations, there are basically three avenues open to couples. Each approach can comprise innumerable variations:

> a) If grounds for annulment exist, the couple can seek a declaration of nullity. The surest grounds for an annulment obtain when God has not joined the couple together (Matt 19:6). From a theological perspective, the two most cogent signs that God has not united a couple are the absence of true love and the lack of a consciousness of an existential inability to be other than married to each other for life.
>
> b) The man and the woman can separate either formally or de facto. That choice may or may not include civil divorce.
>
> c) They may choose to continue living more or less together. Some couples take this third option as the lesser of several evils. They pursue this course for the benefit of their children or for other practical reasons. This avenue preserves the appearance of married life. However, the union is in reality more like cohabitation or coexis-

tence, since each "spouse" lives in effect a separate life. The two "I's" are still two "I's" rather than a "we."

The question then arises: If there is no indication that God is calling a couple to live a married life, is it not hypocritical to go through the motions? Actual situations are never clear-cut. There is always a maze of circumstances. If the couple have children, these are certainly God-given to the two of them. As parents, they have an indissoluble common responsibility. Moreover, there are degrees of affection and a host of other considerations (not the least of which are Canon Law and civil legislation) that bear on the case.

The casuistry and the combinations of possibilities are interminable when one considers failed marriages. It is not our intent to analyze these matters. Our purpose is to offer principles of discernment for authentic callings to married life. We leave the interpretations and the applications of these principles to competent spiritual directors, pastors and counselors.

There is necessarily a legal dimension to marriage, and, therefore, a need for canon lawyers and court proceedings. Yet, there is also a spiritual dimension to wedded life which transcends law. That is the realm of discernment of vocation, of conscience, of faith, hope and love. That spiritual realm is most appropriately addressed by a pastor and above all by a spiritual director.

CELIBATE LIFE

CHAPTER 12

Celibacy: A Personal Consecration

Our vocation to a basic Christian lifestyle is so close to us that it is integral to our personhood. For a long time that calling, though present and operative, remains pre-reflective. We make options in the direction of our vocation, but without adverting to that fact. Only later in life do we recognize the vocational thrust of those decisions. As we work with God to develop ourselves and this world for Christ, our calling to a basic lifestyle evolves and so too does our awareness of it. Eventually, if we are called to marriage or to celibacy, we experience our calling as an existential inability to become otherwise. At that point, we are capable of lifelong commitment.[1]

In this section we explore vocational discernment with regard to celibacy for the sake of Christ and the Gospel.

A. Celibacy: A Personal Calling to a Vocational Lifestyle

Following the episode with the rich young man, Peter poses this question: "What about us, Lord? Since we have given up everything and followed you, what's in it for us?" Jesus replies:

> Whoever has left home . . .
> or wife . . .
> or children . . .
> for my sake and for the sake of the gospel . . .
> receives a hundredfold . . . .[2]

[1]See *Called by God*, 99–112, 115–132.

[2]Matthew 19:29 reads: "houses . . . or children . . . for my name's sake will receive . . . "; Mark 10:29 has: "house . . . or children . . . for my sake and for the sake of the Gospel receives . . . "; Luke 18:29

The most fundamental meaning of that response pertains to evangelical detachment: Everyone is called to relate to the people, the situations and the material objects in one's life as means of transformation rather than as ends in themselves. Evangelical detachment does not necessarily separate a person from those gifts. It corrects within the individual inordinate attachment to them, while preserving a purified—and therefore enhanced—relationship with them. The response of Jesus can be applied to any Christian vocational lifestyle. His invitation to detachment extends to both marriage and singlehood. In the present context, however, we apply Christ's logion to celibacy.

Christian marriage is a distinct sacrament. It comprises a threefold consecration: one spouse to another, each spouse to God, and the wedded unit to God.

Christian celibacy is a personal consecration of an individual to the Lord. It is not a sacrament in its own right, but it brings to fruition in a unique way a person's baptismal and confirmational consecration.

The lifelong commitment of married persons to each other and to God can be *premature* or *mature,* depending on the quality of their vocational consciousness. Those making a mature commitment are aware that the Lord is uniting them for life. On the other hand, those making a premature commitment choose to marry for reasons other than a sense of vocation. Some of these couples discover eventually that God did not unite them and that no interior foundation exists to sustain their juridical bond. Other couples come to recognize that, although they made a precipitous commitment, their initial choice was correct. With more mature consciousness, they ratify their earlier premature decision.

The lifelong commitment to celibacy also can be *premature* or *mature,* depending again on the quality of an individual's vocational consciousness. Those making a mature commitment do so out of a sense of personal vocation to celibacy as a permanent lifestyle. These we shall refer to as *celibate at heart.* Many persons, however, commit themselves prematurely to

---

says: "house or wife . . . or children . . . for the sake of the reign of God . . . receives."

celibacy. These we shall refer to as *celibate by circumstance.* Some of these persons come to realize years later that their initial choice was correct, and they proceed to confirm their earlier decision. Others come to recognize that they had made their decision for reasons other than "for the sake of Jesus and the Gospel" (Mark 10:29). With greater maturity, they see that God is calling them to another vocational lifestyle.

Being celibate at heart lies at the core of several Christian vocations, for example: religious life, monastic life, consecrated virginity, eremitical life. Some people solemnize their celibate commitment with a vow. Others express it more informally by a promise to God or by some other act of personal dedication. In our presentation we prescind from the various expressions of celibate life in order to concentrate on the discernment of a calling to celibacy itself. Thus, in our elaboration of the principles for discernment, we focus on the celibate vocation at its core, irrespective of the specific context in which people live it (religious, clerical, etc.) and regardless of the manner in which they express their commitment (vow, promise, etc.).

The evolution of the consciousness of a calling to celibacy is lengthy and complex. In our presentation, we consider the signs which authenticate the point at which a person experiences a vocation to a celibate lifestyle as an existential inability to become otherwise.

B. The Celibate: Not Just Unmarried, but Unmarriageable

The most commonly recognized logion of Jesus regarding what has come to be known as consecrated celibacy is Matthew 19:12:

> There are eunuchs who are born that way.
> There are eunuchs made so by others.
> And there are those who have made themselves eunuchs
> for the sake of the reign of heaven.
> The person able to receive this,
> receive it.

The Greek text does not speak of the unmarried (*hoi agámoi*), but of the unmarriageable (*hoi eunoúchoi*). Unmarried means quite simply: not married. Unmarriageable, on the other hand, bespeaks inability to marry, incapacity for wedded life. An unmarried person *is not married;* an unmarriageable person *cannot marry.* A single person, therefore, is unmarried but remains quite marriageable. Because the Jews esteemed family life so highly, the label "eunuch" was disgusting and insulting to them.

Although Matthew 19:12 is linked to a teaching about divorce, this logion of Jesus probably originated in a different context.[3] The scribes and the Pharisees had been badgering the Lord for some time about the manner in which he and his disciples distinguished themselves from more orthodox Jews. Jesus and his followers ate with sinners (Mark 2:15-17). They did not keep the Sabbath according to strict pharisaical interpretations (Mark 2:23-28). The Jewish leaders went so far as to denounce Christ as a glutton and a drunkard (Matt 11:19). They noticed also that certain persons had left their spouses and families to follow him. Perhaps some of those antagonists referred sarcastically to the Lord's disciples as "eunuchs"—impotent individuals utterly unfit for marriage.

Responding to their biting remarks, Jesus turned the accusation into a positive way of understanding the celibate calling of some of his disciples. He acknowledged that in a sense certain followers were *eunoúchoi.* Spiritually and vocationally, they were incapable of marriage because of a specific quality in their relationship with him—or, as Matthew put it literally: "for the sake of the reign of the heavens."

In a sense unmarried and unmarriageable represent accents along the same continuum, with multiple shades of grey between them. Both single persons and celibates are unmarried, but the latter are furthermore incapable of marriage. The difference is qualitative as well as relative. Qualitative, because there exists a radical difference between being simply not married and being not able to marry. Relative, because although celibates are vocationally unmarriageable, they may still experience a certain "natural" marriageability as their calling intensifies. Rare is the person who is celibate or who has become aware of him/herself as celibate entirely in one fell swoop. Most people called to the celibate life grow into celibacy as well as

[3]See Edward Schillebeeckx, *Celibacy* (New York: Sheed & Ward, 1968) 21–25, 75–110.

in consciousness of it. In a person basically celibate the perception of a certain marriageability coexisting with unmarriageability becomes especially acute when delayed psychosexual development exists; for example, a celibate in midlife also working through adolescent issues.

C. Celibacy: For the One Called, a Vocational Imperative

In the Greek text, the final phrase of Matthew 19:12 is *ho dynámenos choreín choreíto,* literally: "The [one] being able to receive [it], receive [it]." In the Latin Vulgate, St. Jerome rendered the phrase: *Qui pótest cápere, cápeat:* "Whoever can take it, let him/her take it." *Cápere* means: to take, choose, seize; to take on, receive, undergo; to take in, hold, contain.

Some people have interpreted Jerome's translation along this line: "If you're genitally self-disciplined enough, be celibate. If you can't live without sex, get married." The Greek text, however, is highly nuanced. The verb in question is *choréo,* which is used twice: first, in its infinitive form; second, as a third person singular present imperative. *Choréo* admits of various meanings: to make room (either by motion or capacity); to receive, hold, contain, afford a place to; to go forward, move, proceed, go on; to give (mental) admittance to; to yield in accordance with. It is this final meaning that best suits both the text and context. Thus:

> If the vocation of celibacy has been given to you,
> *yield* to it.
> For ultimately, you can best become yourself in Christ
> by living *in accordance with* the way he is calling you.

Two essential characteristics of the celibate vocation are implied in the last phrase of Matthew 19:12: 1) The person called is not only able, but specifically enabled. It is not so much whether s/he can be celibate, but rather that s/he receives the ability to be celibate. The Lord directly causes and provides the capability. Thus, one's unmarriageability is a necessary effect of having been called by God to celibacy. 2) The main verb in the phrase is in the imperative mood. Thus, having received a celibate vocation, the person is impelled from within to move forward in that direction.

For certain disciples, the experience of Jesus was such that they felt an inner urgency driving them to leave everything, including their homes and families (actual or would-be), in order to follow him. Their encounter with Christ caused not only a personal conversion, but also a new vocational imperative. They had previously enjoyed married or single life. Now, they experience a calling to celibacy. The inner logic of their love for Jesus was such that they found themselves celibate for his sake and for the sake of the Gospel. They necessarily, but freely, had to forego marriage or singlehood. For these disciples, celibacy was a spontaneous result of having found the "hidden treasure," the "pearl of great price" (Matt 13:44-46). For many other disciples, however, their experience of Jesus and the Gospel caused them to remain in their prior lifestyle, but to live it in a Christocentric manner (Acts 4:32-35).

Some people view the celibate consequence of a person's experience of Jesus in an elitist fashion: "If you love him enough, you must be celibate for his sake." In so arguing, they imply that if you are not celibate, it is because you do not love him sufficiently. That interpretation fails to recognize marriage, singlehood and celibacy as vocations in their own right. Each is for the sake of God's reign. For the sake of Christ and the Gospel, Mary and Joseph were called to marriage (Matt 1:18-25) rather than to a celibate lifestyle. Moreover, the proponents of such elitist attitudes fail to appreciate that in the resurrection God transforms not only marriage (Matt 22:23-30), but also celibacy and singlehood.

Nowhere in Scripture does Jesus present celibacy as the ideal for every Christian. Nowhere does he portray it as a calling superior to marriage or singlehood. He does not even imply that it is a universal desideratum. Celibacy is a vocation given to a few. People called to celibacy experience its vocational imperative as flowing from their personal encounter with Christ, similar to the way that married and single persons experience their callings as flowing from their personal encounter with Christ.

In general, how does a *vocational imperative* come about? As we observe people grow in intimacy with God, we notice 1) that their intimacy produces an awareness of a calling to a basic Christian lifestyle. 2) Out of that consciousness arises a certain clarity regarding the fundamental motivation present in choosing one vocation rather than another. 3) That awareness of a calling coupled with relative clarity regarding motivation combine to produce a vocational imperative. Thus, through ever intensifying intimacy with Jesus, a person comes to recognize that s/he must be, for example, celibate, married or single for the sake of Christ and the Gospel.

A vocational imperative to celibacy is at the same time spiritual, ontological and moral.[4] It is a *spiritual imperative* because it is an irresistible movement toward God produced by the Spirit in the deepest recesses of our spirit. As such, it penetrates every facet of our spiritualization. It is also an *ontological imperative* because it is an existential inability to be otherwise. In the realm of being, we best become our transformed selves by way of celibacy. It is furthermore a *moral imperative* because it is an inability to become and to do otherwise. Our lifestyle and our behavior emanate from who God is calling us to be.

The specific imperative toward one basic lifestyle is not of itself more spiritualizing than other vocational imperatives. The imperative produced by each calling is simply different. Thus, when the Lord calls a person to celibacy, the experience of God's love awakens a need in that individual to be celibate rather than married or single. Therefore, let those who have received a vocational imperative to be celibate respond accordingly. By the same token let those who experience another vocational imperative in their encounter with Christ respond accordingly.

Celibacy is a gift freely given to whomever God chooses. So also are marriage and singlehood. For certain persons, celibacy is a commitment of themselves to Jesus through a basic way of life—a lifestyle demanded by the inner logic of their experience of him. Thus: "The person enabled to receive it, receive it" (Matt 19:12).

D. Celibacy: For the Sake of . . .

Matthew 19:12 describes celibacy as being "on account of the reign of heaven." "Reign" in this context indicates a

[4]*Called by God,* 122.

divine-incarnate realm rather than an earthly kingdom. "Of heaven" is a Hebraism denoting the mystery of God within creation. "Reign of heaven" connotes the spiritual, the trans-temporal, the trans-spatial in us and all around us.

Depending on the context, the expression "reign of heaven"—which is synonymous with "reign of God"—refers to the people of God as a whole or to the Lord's activity within an individual.[5] The expression thus conjures up a host of mysteries which theology has come to identify as church, grace, providence, redemption, etc. God's reign comes in the power of the Spirit (Mark 9:1) and is permeated with the glory of the Father (1 Thess 2:12). Who participate in the reign? They are especially "the poor in spirit" (Matt 5:3) and "the persecuted for holiness' sake" (Matt 5:10). These are God's *par excellence.*

Above all, "the reign" refers to the person and the mission of Jesus. His reign has come, is coming and will continue to come. It is even now in our midst, all around us, within us (Luke 17:21). His reign is present, although not yet completely so. It is close at hand, yet eschatological (Mark 1:15). The reign of Jesus is definitely "not of this world" (John 18:36), although it is for the transformation of this world (John 3:16-17).

Celibacy for the sake of "the reign of heaven" (Matt 19:12) is, therefore, not to be understood primarily as a commitment to something, as if to a cause or an ideal. Nor is its main purpose that of building up something, as one would an institution. Authentic celibacy flows out of and redounds to an intimate relationship with Jesus, a loving communion with the person of Christ.

The words of Jesus, "For my sake and for the sake of the Gospel," in Mark 10:29 apply to the motivation underlying a celibate vocation. A love relationship with the Lord is the quintessence and the impetus of the celibate life. Celibates actualize this relationship in two ways: 1) through the progressive surrender of themselves to Christ in faith, hope and love ("for my sake"); and 2) by witnessing to evangelical values ("for the sake of the Gospel"). That witnessing accentuates a qualita-

[5]See *TDNT,* I:564–593.

tive mode of being, a specific Christian lifestyle, a certain way of living out the process of transformation in God.

Since celibacy is both a God-given gift and a consequence of a personal experience of Christ's love, the following sign and condition indicates authenticity: Those called to celibacy encounter Jesus's love for them in such a way that it evokes a celibate response in love. In order to be true to Christ and true to who he is calling them to become, they believe that they must be celibate. The inner dynamics of their relationship with Jesus are such that at some point they experience an existential inability to become themselves in any basic lifestyle except celibacy. In their deepest selves they are impelled in that direction, although on a more superficial level they may experience resistance, fear or ambivalence. They know that for them the peace of Christ lies in voluntary acceptance of their celibate calling.

E. Passage from Singlehood to a Permanent Celibate Commitment

Generally, when people begin thinking even vaguely about vocational lifestyles, they are as a matter of fact single. That means, among other things, that they are unmarried, yet open to and available for marriage. If they are attracted to presbyteral ministry (as it currently exists in the Roman Catholic Church) or to religious life, these persons cannot but notice that those vocations exclude marriage. However, at this early phase of vocational reflection, few persons advert to celibacy as a distinct lifestyle chosen out of a sense of calling.

As a vocation to the presbyterate or the religious life asserts itself in certain people, they enter a seminary or a pre-novitiate program. For the moment, they are in a sense living celibately. That is, although they may not be precisely unmarriageable in the sense described above, they are unmarried and, for the time being, also unavailable for marriage. They are discerning the possibility of a lifelong celibate calling.

If they persevere in one of those vocational directions, these persons are eventually presented for presbyteral ordination or perpetual vows. The moment of truth regarding vocational consciousness has arrived. Juridically, presbyteral ordination (at least for now) and perpetual vows are permanently binding with respect to celibacy. What then is the maturity of the candidate's vocational awareness with regard to celibacy as a lifelong personal calling to an all-embracing and all-penetrating lifestyle?

At this point, people engaged in vocational discernment encounter in candidates variations of the following scenarios:

> 1) God has brought me to mature vocational consciousness. I now experience a calling to celibacy essentially as an existential inability to become otherwise. I am in effect unmarriageable for the sake of Christ and the Gospel (Mark 10:29). Experiencing an ontological, moral and spiritual imperative to commit myself permanently to God as a celibate, I move forward in the living out of that commitment for the rest of my life.
>
> 2) I cannot yet honestly say that I have arrived at an experience of a calling to celibacy as an existential inability to become otherwise. Although I have been living celibately as well as I can, I am not at this time, strictly speaking, unmarriageable for the sake of Christ and the Gospel. However, I believe that God is drawing me in that direction. In the hope that my sense of vocational lifestyle is correct, I will proceed with a lifelong celibate commitment. If I discover later that my decision was a mistake, I will then deal with the situation.
>
> 3) Not only have I not yet arrived at an experience of a calling to celibacy as an existential inability to become otherwise, but I see myself as quite marriageable—even desirous of marriage. I have been living what might be termed "minimal celibacy," that is, I am not presently sexually active. Yet, I feel called to presbyteral ordination or seek full affiliation with a religious institute. Therefore, I choose to assume the juridical obligations of a lifelong celibate commitment, and I hope that my ministry or my liking for this community will sustain indefinitely my sexual abstinence.
>
> 4) Not being able to apply the rudiments of mature vocational consciousness to myself, I choose to put off ordination or perpetual vows for the purpose of further

> discernment. Until I experience the ontological, moral and spiritual imperatives which accompany mature vocational awareness, I will not make a lifelong commitment.

In the last scenario the candidate's reason for delay must be tested. Only if the waiting is discerned to be basically from God and not primarily from other influences would s/he be encouraged to postpone a decision. Some people experience extreme difficulty in making up their minds about anything of consequence. Others are incapable of permanent commitment in any form. Still others tend to put off decisions with long-range effects until they are "absolutely sure," which, for most people, would mean "never." No matter how cogent one's interior imperatives are, lifelong vocational commitment is always a leap in faith.

CHAPTER 13

Celibacy: A Christocentric Commitment

Celibacy is gift. It is a calling to love Christ and to imitate him in a particular way of life. Most persons with a celibate vocation come to awareness of this calling slowly and falteringly. Eventually, however, they arrive at an experience of celibacy as an existential inability to become otherwise. Until they reach that maturity of awareness, permanent commitment would be premature. Moreover, after they have attained that explicit consciousness and have made lifelong commitment, celibates continue to grow in both celibacy and consecration.[1]

Intermingled with the developing consciousness of a vocational imperative, celibates experience also a persistent desire to commit themselves single-heartedly to the person of Jesus. Thus, a second principle for discerning a possible vocation to this basic lifestyle is an irresistible movement toward self-commitment to Christ.

A. Celibacy: An All-Embracing Love Relationship with Jesus

God so loved the world that the Father gave his only Son (John 3:16). That incomprehensible truth expresses in large part how the Father loves us. How then does the Son love us? "As the Father loves me, so I love you" (John 15:9). Jesus loves each person with the same *agápe* with which the Father loves him.

Christ's love for most people is such that it calls them to encounter him through marriage. His love for others is such

[1]See *Called by God,* 141–150.

that it draws them to him through celibacy. His love for still others is such that he invites them to himself through singlehood. At the core of each of these three basic Christian lifestyles is a human love response to a unique experience of Jesus's *agápe*.

Christian celibacy is not primarily a commitment to a value, an ideal, a way or an institution. It is first, foremost and always a consecration of oneself in love to Christ. It is inconceivable that God would call a Christian to lifelong celibacy without gifting that individual with a personal love for Jesus. But how does a celibate love Christ? What quality of *agápe* is necessary to sustain a permanent celibate commitment?

Earlier in this book in the context of marriage (chapter 6), we presented a continuum of human affection in terms of liking, enjoying, caring for, truly loving, loving tenderly and being-in-love. Applying that dynamic to celibacy, it is not enough to like, to enjoy or to care for Jesus. A necessary response to a Christian celibate vocation is true love for him. Integral to the experience of celibacy as an existential inability to become otherwise is the awareness of truly loving Christ and others with some measure of God's own love. Being celibate denotes being empowered by the indwelling Spirit to love the Lord and creation with divine *agápe*. As a person grows into celibacy as well as in consciousness of its vocational dimension, love intensifies, possibly even to the point of being-in-love with Jesus.

In the same chapter on marriage, we used the analogy of friendship to describe developing phases of affective relatedness: a casual friend, a good friend, a close friend, a very special friend, an inseparable friend and the beloved friend. Applying that analogy to a celibate's rapport with Christ, readiness to make a permanent commitment requires at a minimum "a very special" friendship.

A celibate's affective bonding with the Lord is at least as all-embracing as the covenant between two spouses in marriage. No aspect of the celibate's life escapes this intimacy: prayer, relationships, ministry, leisure, study, etc. Jesus himself is thus the immediate source, the sustaining principle and the goal of the celibate's being and becoming.

Therefore, persons discerning a celibate vocation need to

focus on these questions: Do I truly love Christ in a very special friendship? Does my desire for the celibate life and my actual living of this lifestyle flow from and thrust toward ever deepening communion of love with Jesus?

B. Negative and Positive Options for Celibacy

When exploring motives for choosing the celibate life, a logical starting point is the person's attitude toward celibacy itself. Is that attitude basically negative or positive?

A celibate option may be termed "negative" when the underlying motive of the person's choice is not to marry. People elect to remain unmarried for many reasons—some healthy, others unhealthy. In the context of a negative option for celibacy, however, immaturities such as fear and disillusionment or psychological problems such as a Don Juan or a Doña Juana complex generally dominate.[2] Because its inner dynamics remain largely unconscious, a negative option for celibacy is difficult to unmask. Many people in a negative frame of mind think that they are doing just fine.

A positive option for celibacy means choosing this lifestyle because one experiences it as fulfilling. That satisfaction is most meaningful when it flows out of a sense of personal vocation to celibacy for the sake of Jesus and the Gospel (Mark 10:29). In his saying about the "hundredfold" (Matt 19:29; Mark 10:29; Luke 18:29), Jesus implies that celibacy is just as fulfilling to the celibate as marriage is to spouses.

In this life, a celibate's motivation is usually mixed. Positive and negative motives coexist. Therefore, discernment focuses on whether the choice of this lifestyle is *primarily* positive. Even when that is so, not all positive reasons are adequate to sustain a lifelong celibate commitment to God.

C. Inadequate Motives for Assuming Celibacy

Some people do not choose celibacy specifically out of a sense of calling. Reasons other than a vocation emanating from

[2]See Marc Oraison, *The Celibate Condition and Sex* (New York: Sheed & Ward, 1967) 41–87.

intimacy with Jesus prompt them to assume this lifestyle. Many of these persons proceed from false premises. Others emphasize secondary aspects of the vocation to the near exclusion of its primary thrust. Those who base their option for celibacy on an insufficient foundation may be celibate by circumstance but not really celibate at heart.

Four inadequate motives for choosing celibacy are: 1) primarily in view of availability for ministry, 2) mainly as a condition for membership in a religious institute, 3) as a putative source of a more intense relationship with God, and 4) in order to conform to the expectations of others.

1) *Celibacy Principally for the Purpose of Availability for Ministry*

Jesus speaks of those who have left home and children "for my sake and for the sake of the Gospel" (Mark 10:29). "For my sake" refers to evangelical witness in which Christ is the immediate focus. In the present context, we consider that witness in relation to a celibate lifestyle. "For the sake of the Gospel," on the other hand, suggests a ministry which serves an evangelical value—for example, teaching, nursing, service to the poor, the presbyterial office in the Church.

When Jesus insists "for my sake and for the sake of the Gospel" (Mark 10:29), the sequence of those two prepositional phrases is significant. A vocation to celibacy is first, foremost and always for the sake of Christ. God calls a person to leave family, spouse and children directly and primarily for the sake of Jesus. And, because of him, it is also for the sake of the Gospel.

With respect to celibacy and ministry, some people put the cart before the horse. Some who choose presbyterial ordination for the sake of the Lord assume that their accompanying option for celibacy also must be for the sake Christ. Yet, unless they experience a calling to celibacy as well as calling to priestly ministry, their celibate option is for the sake of sacerdotal ordination. If celibacy were not required by Church law, many of them would not embrace it in seeking the presbyterial office.

Celibates at heart experience ministry as integral to their relationship with God. In Christ, they love and serve those to whom the Lord sends them. However, a focus mainly on ministry related to Christ—no matter how excellent—does not suffice of itself to bring a person to celibacy at heart. With this truth in mind, the following question arises in discernment: Does a person's desire to live celibately arise solely or primarily from the attitude that this lifestyle is a convenience or an obligation for the sake of a ministry?

When the underlying reason for a celibate option is convenience or obligation, the motivation is more negative than positive. The would-be celibate is focused more on not marrying for the sake of ministry than on being celibate for the sake of Christ. The person's celibacy is concentrated more on the avoidance of genital intimacies than on the development of the riches of the heart in an affirmation of life and love.

Fundamentally negative motivation, even though well-intentioned, often produces negative effects. Harmony between who I am and how I am becoming myself contributes immensely to my apostolate. When my self-identity is in basic accord with my vocational lifestyle, the quality of my ministry is immeasurably enhanced. The converse is also true. If, for example, I force a celibate life on myself for the sake of a ministry, I could be in effect refusing a calling to marriage or to singlehood. That deprivation could result in an underdeveloped self and an impoverished apostolate.

When people force celibacy on themselves in view of a ministry to which they believe themselves called, they lack a certain at-homeness in their basic lifestyle. They may pursue their apostolate for the sake of Christ, but their way of life remains for the sake of their ministry. That predicament will inevitably affect their apostolate. They will at some point become unable to immerse themselves in their ministry with the life-generating potential that would be theirs if they were living their true vocational lifestyle.

Thus, enforced celibacy begins to work against these persons. Christ in them does not radiate through them and their lifestyle as he could if their mode of living corresponded to their deepest yearnings. These individuals are prone to draw others to themselves rather than to Jesus. Their lack of at-homeness with their basic lifestyle inclines them also to seek out others for noncelibate intimacies or to lose themselves in objects like building projects, rubrics and laws; not to mention alcohol and drugs. Some celibates by circumstance so lack a personal relationship with Jesus that their ministry consists in little more than humanitarian service. We find this especially in those who profess to be celibate, yet claim to have no need of solitude or personal prayer.

Many celibates by circumstance make a sincere effort to foster a personal relationship with the Lord. If God is ultimately calling an individual to celibacy, his/her Christ-centeredness eventually becomes apparent. Regarding celibates by circumstance who are not called to celibacy, the Christocentric aspect of their life also may continue to develop. However, over the course of time many of these persons become aware of a vocation to a different way of life. When they persist in avoiding their calling to another lifestyle—even though actively fostering intimacy with Jesus—these persons become painfully aware that their ministry lacks for them the life-giving quality which it possessed prior to this new sense of direction. Such tension and anxiety takes its toll. Many people trying to live unwanted celibacy become increasingly workaholic; are unable to relax; notice recurring headaches, intestinal disorders or chest pains for which physicians can find no explanation.

In the case of celibacy chosen primarily for ministerial availability, some people argue: "But Christ is in the picture." Perhaps. Yet, unless the Lord is the core of the commitment, experience teaches that one's celibacy will not be a sufficient source of interior growth, nor will celibacy be a meaningful lifestyle. Eventually, the person will have to look elsewhere for fulfillment.

Ministry and lifestyle are two distinct, though not necessarily separate, aspects of vocation. We have to discern each one on its own merits and according to its own principles. Although they remain interrelated, one is not solely, or even primarily, for the sake of the other. Each is for the sake of Christ. Only in Christ do they complement one another.

2) *Membership in a Religious Institute*

Without having experienced an existential inability to become other than celibate, certain people seek for a variety of reasons lifelong membership in religious congregations. Celibacy assumed principally as a condition for membership in a religious community is another inadequate basis for commitment.

Personal commitment to celibacy lies at the core of the religious vocation. Religious life is essentially a community of celibates. A person can be a celibate without being also a religious in the canonical sense, but not vice versa. If God is not calling an individual to celibacy, surely the Lord is not calling that person to a celibate community either. On the other hand, if God is calling an individual to the religious life, then the Lord is necessarily also calling him/her to lifelong celibate consecration. Hence, although clerical celibacy could some day become optional, celibacy in religious life could never be optional.

Religious communities then must discern these questions with regard to their aspirants:

> 1) Is the candidate accepting a celibate way of life primarily as a requirement for association with us? The attitude of the aspirant might go like this: "I have always wanted to be a Franciscan, to wear the habit, to be recognized as a 'poverello.' But celibacy? Well, all right if I must."
>
> 2) Is the person in effect seeking membership in a fraternity or a sorority which happens to be celibate?
>
> 3) Is the aspirant truly seeking to live out a personal celibate commitment to Jesus with the support of other celibates within our institute?

If the response to the first or the second question is affirmative, the fundamental motivation for the celibate option is probably more negative than positive. In reality, the candidate is choosing not to marry—and hence, opting to remain single—rather than to be celibate in the evangelical sense.

In religious formation much emphasis is rightly given to building community. However, some directors assume that because a candidate fits well into the group, s/he possesses a celibate calling. Religious formators have to question the vocation of an aspirant who cannot function in community. But, they have to examine also whether a congenial individual is called by God to celibacy. Many aspirants are relatively easy to get along with and offer considerable promise for a diversity of ministries. Nonetheless, those qualities do not automatically indicate that God is calling these candidates to celibacy.

Discernment of a calling to celibacy and discernment of a vocation to a specific religious institute ordinarily occur simultaneously. However, a certain *order of priority* does exist. There is a certain wisdom to proceeding according to this order:

- First, discern whether the aspirant is indeed called to celibacy rather than to marriage or singlehood.
- Then, discern whether the candidate is called to the religious life in general, for not everyone with a vocation to celibacy is called also to make religious profession.
- Finally, discern whether the aspirant is called to a specific religious charism. There are many congregations and orders in the Church. There are also the canonically recognized individual consecrations of hermit and virgin.

Suppose that in all three discernments the response is affirmative. In this case, the aspirant's basic commitment remains to the person of Christ in and through the institution. Every celibate is for Christ. In him, both the individual and the community are for God and for God's people. Thus, the community is not the celibate's "spouse." Jesus is. The community is not the celibate's "family" either. Father, Son and Spirit are. The religious institute constitutes, however, a unique instrument of God's providence within the celibate's life.

Persons not called to celibacy but who assume a celibate lifestyle as a condition for membership in a religious society experience over time a crippling lack of affirmation and affection. They require something which community cannot furnish. These persons may need a spouse and a family of their own. Lack of affirmation or affection does sometimes arise from dysfunction on the community's part. Yet, if a monk needs a wife or a nun needs a husband, no amount of community—however ideal—will ever suffice.

Both availability for ministry and participation in some form of community are important facets of an integrated celibate life. Yet, neither of those factors constitutes the essence of celibacy. People who persist in the celibate life solely or primarily for those reasons do not find in the long run the nourishment or the fulfillment necessary for growth and perseverance. Moreover, with the true purpose of celibacy overshadowed, the meaning of ministry and community becomes distorted.

3) *A Putative Source of a More Intense Relationship with God*

Some people mistakenly believe that celibacy in itself is a more sanctifying vocation than marriage or singlehood. They think that celibacy is intrinsically a superior state of life. At times, a simplistic interpretation of 1 Corinthians 7:1-40 is used in support of this view. Paul, however, is careful to nuance his response (1 Cor 7:6-7) to the specific question posed to him (1 Cor 7:1). He is furthermore at pains to distinguish what is from the Lord (1 Cor 7:10) from what is his personal opinion (1 Cor 7:25).

Each vocational lifestyle has general advantages and disadvantages. Which way of life has the best advantages in the abstract is not the issue. The crux of the question is a calling from God to a basic lifestyle (1 Cor 7:7). The most advantageous vocation for an individual is the one that God is offering. The lifestyle which most effectively facilitates the person's transformation in Christ is the one that God has chosen for him/her. All abstract advantages and disadvantages pale in comparison to the central issue of the uniqueness of each vocation. What the Lord wills for an individual is not only better, but inevitably best for that person.

> My thoughts are not your thoughts,
>   and my ways are not your ways.
> It is Yahweh who speaks (Isa 55:8).

Emphasis on the celibate "state" over the married and single "states" usually arises out of a static and compartmentalized world view. From an evolutionary and relational perspective, it is more accurate to speak of dynamic ways of life, of developing lifestyles—all of which in themselves are equally effective milieus of God's transforming and purifying activity.

4) *Conformity to Others' Expectations*

At times, pressure—real or imagined—from significant persons drives people to do things that they would not otherwise undertake. There are persons who try to live celibately in order to conform to the expectations of parents, family or an idealized religious. In some instances, childhood and adolescence are little more than home postulancies. Certain formators hold such power over candidates that they mold them into "good little celibates," regardless of their vocation. Needless to say, a rude awakening lies in store.

Family tradition exerts a special kind of moral pressure. Perhaps one has an older brother or sister already in religious life. Now, either in imitation of or in competition with him/her, the younger sibling seeks to be celibate as well. If that is the dominant motivation, this person is ill-equipped to persevere.

D. Other Counterindications of a Christocentric Focus

The person of Jesus is the alpha, the omega and the raison d'être of a commitment to evangelical celibacy. In addition to the above inadequate motives, certain other situations indicate a possible defect in Christocentric focus. These are especially: 1) lack of sufficient self-identity, 2) negative attitudes toward marriage, 3) externalism in prayer, and 4) an excessive desire for security. When a person vows celibacy before resolving these issues, s/he is probably celibate by circumstance rather than celibate at heart.

1) *Lack of Sufficient Self-Identity*

Basic self-identity, healthy self-love and adequate self-knowledge are prerequisites for an authentic celibate commitment. Without them, a person does not possess sufficient interior freedom for self-commitment to Christ through celibacy. Ordinarily, a man or a woman who comes to the experience of a calling to celibate life for the sake of Jesus and the gospel has already developed a strong self for Christ.[3]

That self-development occurs through interpersonal relationships, work, study, socializing, dating, loving and being loved. Through these means the person collaborates with God

[3]See *Contemplation,* 116–121; *O Blessed Night,* 132–137; *Receptivity,* 85–88; *Spiritual Journey,* 55–74.

in forming a self that is psychologically, emotionally, sexually and spiritually integrated.

Some obvious questions arise: Does the prospective celibate have an adequate sense of personal identity? Does the candidate possess mature self-love and self-confidence? Does the aspirant have enough self-knowledge and experience of Jesus to freely choose a celibate way of life? Is the person's psychosexual development sufficient?[4]

2) *Negative Attitudes Toward Marriage*

The prospective celibate's stance toward marriage is significant. Does the attraction to celibacy arise from negative attitudes toward married life? Misdirection of this kind can originate in the experience of an unhappy or a broken marriage between one's parents. Is fear of making a marital commitment a motivating factor? Is the person seeking to escape the responsibilities of family life? Does the desire for celibacy stem from a tendency to avoid the self-donation and self-denial necessarily involved in a marital relationship?

3) *Externalism in Prayer*

The core of a vigorous prayer life is a personal response in faith, hope and love to the indwelling Father, Son and Spirit. Is the prospective celibate's prayer centered around the fulfillment of external religious practices? Does the candidate engage in formal prayer to the exclusion of personal and solitary prayer? Or are the externals of the candidate's prayer life a true expression of an interior loving communion with Jesus?

4) *Excessive Desire for Security*

The prospect of a certain spiritual, emotional or material security attracts some people to the celibate life, especially as it is lived in religious institutes. Is the prospective celibate seeking a safe haven rather than a life of faith-filled risk and detachment for the sake of Christ? Is the aspirant trying to secure heaven by circumventing the world? Does the candidate shirk

[4]See Oraison, *The Celibate Condition,* 15–87; Michael Cavanagh, "The Impact of Psychosexual Growth on Marriage and Religious Life," *Human Development* 4 (3, 1983) 16–24; Erik Erikson, *The Life Cycle Completed* (New York: Norton, 1982) 25–53.

responsibility for his/her personal life under a naive notion of religious obedience? Does the would-be celibate want those in authority to make all significant decisions so that s/he can avoid the possibility of making a mistake?

CHAPTER 14

The Holistic Orientation of Celibate Life

By its very nature a calling to a Christian lifestyle tends to enhance overall development of the individual. In some way and to some measure, each vocational lifestyle contributes to growth in all aspects of personhood—emotional, social, psychosexual, spiritual, etc.

Celibacy is holistic inasmuch as it promotes the human development and the spiritual maturity of those so called by God. The celibate mode of life becomes imperative for certain people because of the way they experience loving communion with the Trinity. That imperative fosters in them ever deeper love for God and creation. It penetrates every facet of daily existence. All dimensions of the celibate life interact to form a milieu for intensifying encounter with God and creatures.

Thus, the experience of celibacy as holistic is another positive sign of a possible vocation. It takes a prolonged period of actually living celibately before a candidate can discern whether this lifestyle in fact promotes overall integration. A person has to grow into a holistic experience of celibacy. Yet, before permanent commitment to God through celibacy, there needs to be convincing indication that the candidate has attained a basic threshold of holistic maturity.

In this chapter, we examine three expressions of the holistic orientation of celibate life which bear significantly on vocational discernment. They are: integration, need for solitude and practice of celibate chastity.

A. Integration

Continuous communion with the indwelling Father, Son and Spirit is the basic integrating principle in the life of every Christian.[1] A person's loving communion with God in solitude of heart integrates all the diverse elements of daily living: apostolic involvement, study, recreation, personal relationships, exterior solitude, communal or familial interaction, solitary prayer, public prayer, etc. A celibate witnesses in his/her own specific manner to that truth.

To integrate means to blend different aspects of a reality into a whole, to incorporate parts into a larger unit. Integration implies harmony, balance, consolidation—getting it all together. Integration does not, however, suggest absence of tension. A certain tension is necessary for the balancing of converging elements. Moreover, because the precise manner of establishing a balance varies constantly, there must be ongoing discernment, flexibility and willingness to change. The nuances of God's calling unfold gradually through all the developing circumstances of our lives.

Positive indication of a vocation to celibate life includes the candidate's experience of continuous communion with Jesus, together with the realization that all dimensions of daily life are drawn into that intimate encounter. The aspirant's ability to accept the normal tension which goes with the integration process is a further confirmation of a possible celibate vocation. Those involved in the discernment, however, need to be alert to the presence of undue tension. Unhealthy stress in the candidate could be evident in the following: compulsiveness in work, study, eating or drinking; excessive concern over health; mental scatteredness; preoccupation with a certain recreational activity; engrossment in personal relationships; dichotomy between prayer and activity or between solitude and communal life.

When celibates lack integration in their prayer life or when areas of undue tension persist, they need to discern the origin of the difficulties. It may be that there is no calling at all to celibate life. Or possibly God is not yet calling them to celi-

[1]See *Contemplation,* 125–140.

bate commitment, but with time will bring them to it. Perhaps the incongruity stems from an obstruction in personal growth that needs correction irrespective of lifestyle.

Celibate integration must be especially evident in the candidate's experience of him/herself as interiorly whole and psychosexually fulfilled without having a lifelong partner and a family of his/her own. A celibate is not only unmarried, but also unmarriageable. Yet, that absence of marriage does not constitute a deprivation of something essential for a celibate's personal integration. Furthermore, wholeness for the celibate does not require the type of independence which a person called to singlehood experiences. To be whole, a celibate needs a particular quality of solitude.

B. Need for Solitude

Since union in love with Jesus remains the crux of Christian celibate life, solitude is essential to vibrant celibacy.

This solitude is above all an interior solitude. Therein the celibate abides intentionally with the Lord in loving communion (John 15:4-5). That communion persists whether the celibate is praying or working, alone or with people, recreating or sleeping. Through interior solitude the celibate grows ever more conscious of the mystery of Christ becoming "all in all" (1 Cor 15:28; Col 3:11) and especially all in his/her own life (Gal 2:20).

Continuous prayer of the heart does not cause a cleavage between the celibate's communion with Christ and the particulars of daily existence. On the contrary, communion intensifies in and through the activity at hand. Attentiveness of mind and heart to the present moment fosters an integrated prayer life.

Nonetheless, it is difficult, if not impossible, to commune continuously in interior solitude with Jesus without some daily exterior solitude. All persons—but especially celibates—need to set aside for a while each day their usual responsibilities and diversions in order to focus directly on their Beloved.

> [Jesus himself] would always go off to some solitary place where he could be alone and pray (Luke 5:16).

The amount of exterior solitude requires ongoing discernment in the light of one's vocational responsibilities.[2] However, many celibates shortchange themselves, God and their mission by spending too little time in solitary prayer.

A person who is celibate at heart experiences the need for both interior and exterior aloneness with God. For a celibate, solitude is as necessary for spiritual growth as rest is for the body and the psyche. Celibates sometimes resist seeking out aloneness with God or try to evade solitude when it is available. Inevitably, however, they find peace only by acquiescing to it. An increasing desire for solitude accompanies growth in celibacy. The more a couple advance in love, the more they need to be together. Similarly, the more a person becomes celibate—even if s/he is an extreme extrovert—the more that person desires to be alone with God for extended periods.

Remaining alone with Jesus daily is necessary for intimate communion. Can the prospective celibate stand being alone with Christ? Does the aspirant experience a need to be alone with God? Is the candidate at home with solitary prayer?

Absence of the desire and the ability to secure personal solitude casts doubt on the authenticity of a celibate vocation.

C. Practice of Celibate Chastity

Chastity is integral to every Christian's relationship with Jesus. The virtue of chastity helps people to moderate according to their vocation sexual desires and the expression of them. As God calls married partners to conjugal chastity and single persons to single chastity, so the Lord calls celibates to celibate chastity. These three signs offer positive indication that a person possesses the maturity necessary to practice celibate chastity:

1) *The candidate has proven him/herself capable of practicing chastity in the single life.*

Celibacy is not an escape for one who cannot otherwise moderate sexual impulses. Some people naively imagine that the solution to a problem of promiscuity in the single life is

[2]See ibid., 126–131.

to make a vow of celibacy. If promiscuity remains unresolved in singlehood, it will present itself with equal, if not greater, force in the celibate life.

2) *In the area of psychosexual development, the aspirant is at home with his/her sexual identity and orientation.*

The candidate needs to know whether s/he is basically heterosexual, homosexual or bisexual. Moreover, the candidate has to have made peace with that knowledge. It is also necessary that the person confront any inclinations toward fetishism, transvestism, zoophilia, pedophilia, exhibitionism, voyeurism, masochism, sadism and the like. A marked tendency toward any of those sexual addictions in a person considering celibacy requires professional evaluation over a prolonged time.

A homosexual or a bisexual orientation does not of itself rule out a possible calling to celibacy for the sake of Christ and the Gospel. However, in-depth vocational discernment can begin only with the person's explicit acceptance of that homosexual or bisexual disposition and with realistic acknowledgement of the difficulties entailed in living closely with celibates of the same sex.

A person with a homosexual orientation who has an authentic vocation to celibacy is called to be celibate at heart and not merely celibate by circumstance. Thus, the candidate and his/her spiritual guides must consider to what extent any of the following motivations affect the option for celibacy: lack of attraction toward marriage; effort to squelch a longing to enter an active homosexual relationship; desire to hide homosexuality under the guise of a socially acceptable lifestyle. The candidate has to have also developed the skills necessary to contend with difficulties associated with a homosexual orientation, for example: low self-esteem, guilt feelings, homophobic biases, a personal sense of rejection by much of society and the Church.

A person with a bisexual orientation who has a vocation to celibacy also is called to be celibate at heart and not merely celibate by circumstance. In a climate where sexual orientation is generally polarized into heterosexuality and homosexuality, bisexuality strikes many—even the well educated and the tolerant—as an enigma and a discomfort. When a person's bisexual orientation becomes known, s/he often meets with confusion and repulsion in both straight and gay friends. A bisexual celibate must be able to deal constructively with this anxiety and hostility.

3) *The aspirant has passed through the stages of psychosexual development which precede the norm for his/her chronological age.*[3]

Some difficulties relating to celibate chastity stem from retarded psychosexual development. Despite advanced chronological age and intelligence, a candidate may be adolescent or even preadolescent with regard to psychosexual growth.

Take the example of a woman who as a youth entered the convent directly from a very sheltered and controlled environment. During adolescence and early adulthood, she had little or no opportunity to explore her femininity in relation to the opposite sex. She did not date or interact sufficiently with boys on a peer basis. Then at midlife she experiences herself as woman in the eyes of a man. Although she is mature in other respects, she may still be adolescent in relation to the masculine. Since nature tends to correct itself, both adolescent and midlife psychosexual issues will likely assert themselves. Either set of issues is challenging enough at its appropriate time. But both concomitantly and out of usual sequence can give rise to considerable anxiety.

To become capable of mature heterosexual encounter, this woman has to pass through her delayed adolescence. In doing so, much of what she was taught to consider as temptation may be in reality struggles normal to her stage of psychosexual development. The woman and her spiritual guides need first to identify the issue correctly. Rather than immediately trying to determine whether a specific difficulty indicates absence of a call to celibacy, they have to approach the struggle as a normal, although delayed, aspect of psychosexual development which is now running its course. The

[3]See Michael Cavanagh, "The Impact of Psychosexual Growtn on Marriage and Religious Life," *Human Development* 4 (3, 1983) 16–24; Erik Erikson, *The Life Cycle Completed* (New York: Norton, 1982) 25–53.

implications regarding a celibate vocation will unfold in due time. The aspiring celibate and her spiritual guides can then consider those implications in the light of the other principles for discernment.

Patience, understanding, leisure, self-acceptance, perseverance, solitude are essential dispositions for persons working through delayed psychosexual development. Until the candidate has caught up to the norm for his/her chronological age, permanent commitment is inadvisable. In the case of individuals who have already made perpetual vows, resolution of the delayed psychosexual issues best precedes recommitment to celibacy.

A candidate or a spiritual director may identify as vocational crisis what is really a crisis related to a stage of spiritual growth or of psychological maturation. Here are two examples: 1) In the night of sense as one encounters God more directly and immediately, intense storms and trials arise from the concupiscible appetite. St. John of the Cross refers to that paradox as "the spirit of fornication."[4] Confused and anxious, the person may think that those intense urges indicate lack of a celibate vocation. 2) As an unmarried person approaches midlife, it is normal to reevaluate basic life choices and to experience at times increased longings for a marital relationship as well as for children. A celibate on the verge of midlife could misinterpret those longings which arise from a healthy aging process as being indicative of a calling to marriage.

Prospective celibates, as well as their spiritual directors, have to discern the origin of any difficulty with regard to chastity. Is it indicative of a genuine vocational crisis? Or is it primarily the result of passage through a developmental threshold of psychological or spiritual growth? The primary source of the struggle can be difficult to identify. In many instances, both vocational crisis and passage through a developmental stage occur simultaneously. A vocational crisis does not, however, always augur a change from one vocational lifestyle to another. Such crises can serve as catalysts for a deeper and more realistic commitment in one's present calling.

[4]*The Dark Night of the Soul*, 1, 14, 1. See *Contemplation*, 85–96; *O Blessed Night*, 79–87; *Receptivity*, 39–41; *Spiritual Journey*, 108–113, 171–172.

CHAPTER 15

The Celibate as Solitary

A vocation to the celibate life implies a calling to be a solitary person. The celibate's all-embracing relationship with Jesus causes him/her to be alone to a significant degree.

However, the solitariness of celibacy consists of more than the usual Christian need to imitate Jesus by going apart periodically to some secluded place in order to be alone and pray (Luke 5:16). The celibate shares that need with married and single persons as well. Besides calling celibates to solitary prayer, God calls them also to be solitary persons, even if they are naturally gregarious and extroverted.

Failure to integrate the solitary dimension of celibate life leads to excesses such as alcoholism, drug addiction, rugged individualism, extreme legalism, sexual promiscuity, outright meanness toward others.

Thus, the experience of being solitary constitutes an important principle in the discernment of a possible vocation to celibacy.

A. The Awareness of Being a Solitary

Celibates at heart are solitaries in a twofold sense. Interiorly, God calls them to commune in loving receptivity with the indwelling Trinity. Exteriorly, God calls them to a certain aloneness in relation to other people. Because of Christ and the gospel, it becomes impossible for a celibate to share his/her whole self and life with another person. S/he must leave "brothers, sisters, father, mother, children," (Mark 10:29) and "spouse" (Luke 18:29) as a consequence of the Lord's calling.

The celibate is thus drawn to radical exterior as well as interior detachment.

The aloneness of a celibate is not isolation or withdrawal. Isolation or withdrawal means cutting oneself off from God and creation. It is a narcissistic turning in upon self and impedes human development. Integral to the celibate's solitariness is an opening up of self to God and others. That aloneness paradoxically forms the milieu in which the celibate's communion with the Lord and others intensifies. Solitude, or remaining alone with God, is fraught with potential for growth and altruism.[1]

The celibate experiences aloneness in the midst of the world primarily in these two ways: by involvement with creation and by the foregoing of marriage and family life.

1) *Involvement with Creation*

Involvement with creatures—the highlight of which is interpersonal relationships—opens the celibate to solitude. The fulfillment and success, the satisfaction and enjoyment, as well as the pain and suffering of that involvement inevitably lead the celibate to radical aloneness.

Through interaction with creation, the celibate learns this truth: I am other than everything and everyone else. I am responsible for my life, my choices and my decisions. No one else can live my life for me. I can give back to God and to the world something which no other creature can. My love for other persons and their love for me point me beyond them to God. Through those people God opens me to search for the "I-don't-know-what behind their stammering."[2] Moreover, the powerlessness and helplessness which I experience when I suffer also contain an invitation to be more abandoned to the Lord alone.

In other words, through involvement with creation the celibate tastes an inability to be completely satisfied by anyone or anything except God.[3] As a normal consequence of his/her joys and sufferings, the celibate enters a sometimes frightful

[1]See *Contemplation,* 98–99; *Spiritual Journey,* 62–71.

[2]St. John of the Cross, *The Spiritual Canticle,* stanza 7.

[3]See *O Blessed Night,* 47–68; *Receptivity,* 17–31; *Contemplation,* 62–65.

abyss wherein s/he stands alone before God. There the celibate experiences insatiable longing and thirsting for the Lord. Every person undergoes that yearning sooner or later, but one called to celibacy does so specifically *as a celibate.*

2) *The Foregoing of Marriage and Family*

Foregoing matrimony and the opportunity to establish a family confronts the celibate with a particular kind of aloneness. Whereas in marriage a person enters a partnership of love, in the celibate life one lives with a certain physical, emotional and psychological separateness. Because of a sense of calling, there exists a voluntary lack of conjugal intimacy and family life. Because of Christ and the Gospel, there is no husband or wife, no children or grandchildren. The vocational absence of that kind of loving and belonging produces a unique form of emptiness, aloneness and rootlessness.

Many persons view such absence as privation. Absence means simply not being there. Privation, on the other hand, denotes the lack of something which should be there. Not having blue eyes would be an absence. Losing one's sight would be a privation. For a true celibate, foregoing marriage and the opportunity to establish a family is an absence, not a deprivation. The emptiness, aloneness and rootlessness spring from a positive source and lead to holistic growth. Yet, the manner in which a celibate experiences solitude ranges from turmoil to peace, from loneliness to solidarity, from anguish to joy.

Some celibates attempt—whether consciously or unconsciously—to squelch their yearnings for a family of their own with community interaction. Membership in a vibrant community remains an invaluable help to any celibate. Yet, one's community is not, strictly speaking, one's family. Community is meant to be a positive support and challenge, not an emotional substitute or an affective scapegoat.

In the case of the religious life, community is sometimes compared with family—a religious family. That image has value as long as it remains analogous. A religious community is first and foremost a community of celibates who participate in the charism of a specific institute. Neither religious life in general nor a community in particular can effectively become a surrogate family for its members. Nothing takes the place of the family which celibates are called to forego, and nothing can substitute for the solitude which they must undergo. The person of Jesus remains the prime focus and sole *raison d'être* of the celibate life.

While the call to celibacy renders a person unmarriageable, many celibates possess an abundance of qualities necessary for successful marriage and parenting. Were it not for Christ and the Gospel, these celibates would like very much to marry and to raise a family. Moreover, they would be excellent at it. They have the ability and the need to love and to be loved, the capacity to be faithful to another person, the willingness to give generously of themselves. Thus, a paradoxical element in many celibates' *existential inability* to be otherwise is paradoxically their *natural potential* to be otherwise. That situation becomes a powerful sign that their unmarriageability is not from any source but the Lord:

> We are only earthenware jars which hold this treasure
> to make it clear that the excellence of this power
> comes from God and not from us (2 Cor 4:7).

Long after mature vocational consciousness and permanent commitment, these celibates continue to have a natural potential for marriage and perhaps at times a strong attraction toward married life. Nevertheless, they see that their most profound need and desire is to remain celibate. The call to celibacy resonating from within the deepest recesses of their being is unmistakable. At that depth, what God wills and what they will converge.

The gist of the celibate experience is this: As a consequence of Christ's love for me and of my love for him, I have to be celibate. I truly want to pursue this path, even though I have an attraction and a capacity for a conjugal relationship and family life.

The positive and creative aspects of the tension between the call to celibacy and the potential for marriage are not always apparent to the person undergoing it. At times, the tension lies dormant and poses no particular threat. At other times, it emerges with moderate intensity. On occasion, it assails with frightening force.

It is especially in the last instance that celibates experience the full brunt of their inner poverty. They cannot persevere in celibacy on willpower and good intention alone. If they are celibate at heart, out of their experience of weakness emerges a heightened consciousness of the mystery of God's calling:

> You did not choose me;
> No, I chose you (John 15:16).

Celibates thus discover that while they can do nothing of themselves, they can do all things in God who empowers them (Phil 4:13). They become more aware not only that their calling is pure gift, but also that they receive even their ability to respond positively to it. Paradoxically, as celibates experience ever more profoundly their poverty of spirit, they grow in consciousness of their vocation and in freedom to lovingly surrender themselves to Jesus.

B. The Celibate's Sacrifice of the Potential for Marriage

Every celibate has to grapple at one time or another with these questions: Why has God chosen me, such an inept person, for celibacy? Why did the Lord give me all this capacity for wedded life and then not call me to use it?

The biblical notion of sacrifice sheds some light on those enigmatic questions. To sacrifice something to God is to do or to refrain from doing something which apart from love and a sense of calling one would never engage in or abstain from. Thus, according to Hebrew custom, heifers in their prime and the first fruits of the harvest were to be offered to the Lord. To sacrifice them in this manner was to use them eminently. From a pragmatic viewpoint, such practice is sheer stupidity. It would be far more sensible to sell the best cattle and to offer up the barren and diseased animals. It would be far more reasonable to market the first corn and wheat, sacrificing the leftovers to the Lord. After all, God eats neither meat nor grain.

However, God bestows some gifts in order to have them sacrificed and thus used eminently. The Servant of Yahweh lamented:

> The Lord has made my mouth a sharp sword,
> yet hid me in the shadow of God's hand.
> The Lord formed me into a piercing arrow,
> yet concealed me in God's quiver (Isa 49:2).

Yahweh had given the Servant certain talents which he was not permitted to use in a pragmatic way. Why be given such a gift? Using reasonableness as his standard, the Servant concluded:

> I have toiled in vain,
> wasted my energy for nothing (Isa 49:4).

Conventional wisdom judges as useless and frustrating something which cannot produce fruit. Yet, the truth of the matter can be just the opposite. The Servant did employ those gifts in Yahweh's service, although in a way that conventional wisdom would not recognize or deem productive:

> The Lord insisted: "You are my servant
> in whom I am glorified" . . .
> For my cause was with Yahweh,
> my reward with my God (Isa 49:3-4).

To sacrifice to God gifts from God when the Lord calls us to do so is to use them in a transcendent manner. Thus, persons who sacrifice their potential for marriage because of a vocation to celibacy do use that God-given ability, but in a way that defies logic and practicality. They use it eminently and transcendently. Moreover, the more fully human the celibate becomes, the richer the self-sacrifice to the Lord.

How do celibates deal with their sexual desire and natural ability to found a family? Not by repression, but by sublimation. To sublimate comes from two Latin words meaning to polish the underneath of something—in other words, to do such a thorough job that even the underside comes out sparkling. To sublimate denotes diverting an appetite or an impulse from its usual course to one more desirable in the light of a personal calling. Sublimation in this sense is integral to every Christian lifestyle.

A basic challenge for celibates then is to accept their radical aloneness and their humanness, including all its potential to be other than celibate. Because of their vocation, aloneness and humanness contain an invitation to ever deeper encounter with God.

Many celibates experience temptations to escape solitude or to indulge in humanness. Some succumb to those temptations by filling up their lives with egocentric relationships, dissipating diversions or feverish business. Others capitulate to those allurements by abusing meaningful friendships, by overdoing helpful diversions or by taking on excessive ministerial activity.

What appear as negative effects of foregoing marriage (emptiness, barrenness, loneliness, insufficient intimacy, etc.) can be in reality effective means by which God opens celibates to divine life.

> My power is at its best in weakness (2 Cor 12:9).

In this poverty, there is nowhere to turn except to Jesus (John 6:68). Thus, being without roots in a marital sense is for those called to celibacy an integral aspect of their pilgrimage in faith. It affords the opportunity for them to discover that they belong to God alone.

C. Two Different Experiences of the Potential for Marriage

The manner in which celibates at heart undergo their natural potential for married life differs radically from the way in which celibates by circumstance experience that capacity.

Celibates at heart see their capacity for marriage as an aspect of their humanness which is integrable with their commitment to Christ. Even after the emergence of consciousness of a call to celibacy as an existential inability to become otherwise, a celibate's natural attraction toward marriage could at some time produce a vocational crisis. In that case, however, the person will emerge from the struggle even more acutely aware of a vocation to celibacy and more at peace with this calling.

Celibates by circumstance, on the other hand, experience the situation quite differently. Celibates at heart have already a definite sense of vocation. Celibates by circumstance are still searching interiorly to discover their calling. A vocational crisis for the former tends to strengthen that which is already conscious. A vocational crisis for the latter occasions an awakening which may or may not be consistent with the person's current direction. Attraction toward marriage can indicate to the celibate by circumstance that married life is indeed his/her calling. Yet, it can have the opposite effect too. For in grappling with the viable possibility of a vocation to marriage, the celibate by circumstance may experience an unequivocal calling to celibacy. Should a celibate by circumstance discern at this juncture a calling to marriage or to the single life, s/he has not lost his/her vocation, but rather discovered an essential dimension of it.

Instances of celibacy by circumstance are extremely complex and need to be considered on an individual basis. Whatever the particulars, however, while celibates by circumstance are trying to follow Christ as best they can, God's providence is operative on their behalf.[4] For example, a woman's fifteen years in the convent are not wasted in terms of spiritual development for either herself or others. The Lord incorporates all that time and effort into the process of her awakening to her basic vocational lifestyle.

Some celibates by circumstance who are "in vows" assume that they are interiorly consecrated by reason of the profession ceremony which they underwent in good faith. Only later do they realize otherwise. The problem underlying this situation is often the formation systems through which these persons pass. Many institutions do not challenge their candidates with sufficient directness and depth on the issue of celibacy. Moreover, some formators do not have the patience or the procedures to wait for God to bring forth in aspirants to the celibate life a mature vocational consciousness. They push candidates along, without taking the time or ensuring the freedom required for decisive vocational discernment.

In discerning their vocational lifestyles, celibates by circumstance as well as their spiritual guides have to be completely open to the outcome. On the part of celibates by circumstance, fear of taking necessary risk, fear of letting go the familiar, fear of the unknown, fear of not measuring up to the expectations of others can greatly impede openness. Spiritual guides, for

[4]See *Spiritual Journey*, 19–32; *Called by God*, 9–35.

their part, can lack the necessary receptivity by proceeding in discernment from the assumption that God could not possibly be calling an individual whom they care for and admire to anything but the celibate life.

CHAPTER 16

The Celibate in Relation to Community

An authentic celibate is by vocation a solitary person. Yet, the celibate's aloneness with God is the milieu in which s/he enters into profound communion and community with many others.

Family life is integral to marriage. Participation in community is integral to celibacy. Celibate community can consist of living together under the same roof, as in a religious house. It can also mean living alone while preserving a bond with a congregation or loosely-knit community of believers. Community for a celibate can be composed of same sex members. Or it can be mixed, as in some Houses of Prayer where membership is open to men and women, married, single or celibate.

In this chapter, we discuss the communal dimension of celibate life. We focus on two principles of discernment: first, the community of Father, Son and Spirit as the source of Christian community; second, Christian community as participation in the community of the Trinity.

A. The Community of Father, Son and Spirit

Christian community is sometimes described in terms of praying together, sharing the same ministry, living in common, forming a brotherhood or a sisterhood. Depending on one's vocation, any of those elements can constitute a valid aspect of communal life. However, in-depth community can be lacking even when those components are present. Community can also exist without any of those factors. The most striking example of the latter is the eremitical life. While living, praying and working alone, a hermit participates profoundly in community.

To explore the mystery of community, we look to the community of the Trinity. All Christian community has its source in God's inner life. Jesus prayed that all his disciples be one, just as Father, Son and Spirit are one:

> May they all be one, Father,
> as you are in me and I am in you . . .
> May they be one in us . . .
> as we are one (John 17:21-22).

With regard to the community of the Trinity, we highlight these features: solitude, unity, differentiation, creation by God and recapitulation of all in Christ.

1) *Solitude*

Solitude denotes being alone with God. The interrelatedness of the divine persons within the Trinity involves a certain solitude. The Father remains alone with the Son and the Son remains alone with the Father, each loving the other. In love, the Father and the Son spirate the Spirit. The Spirit in turn abides in solitude with the Father and the Son.

2) *Unity*

Solitude tends to unite. The solitude of each divine person is intimately related to the unicity of God. Alone with each other, Father, Son and Spirit are so united in love that there is but one God.

3) *Differentiation*

Love differentiates as it unites. The union of the divine persons in solitude differentiates each person. It enhances what most uniquely constitutes the Father as Father, the Son as Son and the Spirit as Spirit.

4) *Creation and Recapitulation of All in Christ*

The communion of Father, Son and Spirit is such that God's love diffuses itself. God thus brings into being and indwells creation. That creative diffusion of God's love is in process. It is causing creation to become what it is meant to be. Creating, God moves the human person from immaturity to maturity, from scatteredness to completion. Indwelling, God transforms and divinizes the person. The process of uniting or recapitulating all creation in Christ (Col 1:15-20; 3:11) we call Christification. The process of perfecting the human person in God we name deification.

B. Christian Community

Solitude, communion in love, differentiation, creation and recapitulation are fundamental qualities of Trinitarian community. Since Christian community is a participation in the community of Father, Son and Spirit (John 17:23), those qualities form the foundation of Christian community.

1) *Solitude*

As paradoxical as it may seem at first, solitude is the basis of all indepth Christian community. To the extent that a person accepts his/her aloneness with God, that individual is capable of more qualitative communion with others. To the degree that a person communes in solitude with Father, Son and Spirit, s/he is in spiritual union with the local community, with the whole Church, indeed with the entire universe. To the depth that a person abides in the Trinity—the source, the sustenance and the goal of all—s/he abides in communion with all.

Prospective celibates, therefore, need to discern the following questions: Do I experience solitude as communion with God and others? Have I come to recognize the profound relationship of solitude to community?

2) *Union with Creation in God*

Participation in the community of the indwelling Trinity necessarily opens us to all creation. We cannot love God without also loving our neighbor (1 John 4:20-21). Love for God and love for others are two aspects of the same mystery: our participation in God's love.

Why is that so? It is because in God we encounter all: everything and everyone. Apart from God there is nothing (John 15:5). In God, we live and move and have our being (Acts 17:28). In God, we encounter what is deepest in one another. In God, the Spirit forms us into one body, the Body of Christ, his *ekklesía*—that is, his assembly, his congregation, his people, his Church, his community (Eph 3:21).

Our union with one another in God respects the sentiments characteristic of each of our loves. We do not merely love all people in a general way. Rather, community in Christ consists of particular relationships, each with its own joys and sorrows, strengths and weaknesses, successes and failures. Each of those love relationships is itself undergoing a process of transformation and purification.

Christian celibacy is not withdrawal or isolation from the world. God calls the celibate, like every other Christian, to detachment with regard to everyone and everything created. Yet, that detachment enables the celibate to enjoy all creatures with unrestricted freedom of spirit. Celibacy calls an individual to develop the riches of the heart. It is an affirmation of life and love. It invites the person to become more human, sensitive and affectionate. Instead of cutting one off from the world, celibacy is a means of communing with Christ and with all creation in him at the very heart of the world.[1]

Thus, the solitary quality of celibate life is not in opposition to intimacy in relationships. On the contrary, it calls forth mature involvement. Just as one cannot have intimacy with others without some solitude, neither can one have any depth of solitude without experiencing some intimacy. Tension between solitude and human intimacy is normal. However, excessive conflict between the two is usually a sign of an inordinate attachment or distorted attitude within the celibate.

Discrepancy between the mode of intimacy to which God calls them and the expression of intimacy for which they yearn produces sometimes intense conflict in celibates. They become discontent with what will ultimately bring them personal fulfillment and happiness in light of their vocation. God seems emotionally distant and too intangible. The lack of satisfaction tempts them to seek relief: in a bottle, from a syringe, with a warm body, etc. Losing sight of the intimacy that is already present or at least possible within their celibate life, conjugal intimacy may have an almost overwhelming appeal. Yet, if as-

[1]See *O Blessed Night*, 47–68, 158–163, 171–177; *Receptivity*, 17–31, 109–112, 114–120.

suaging their emptiness is the prime motivation in their attraction toward matrimony, that direction too is sadly distorted.

Candidates for the celibate life, therefore, need to discern these questions: Just what are my expectations of community? Am I demanding that my community be a substitute for my would-be family? Am I relatively content with the intimacy possible in celibate life, or do I need marital intimacy? Am I a loving person who is willing to risk forming deep friendships with both men and women? Am I willing to let myself be vulnerable, even to the point of being hurt occasionally? Or am I isolated, cut off from affection, withdrawn from others? Am I spending my time catering to my egocentric interests and concerns?

3) *Diversity in Community*

Our communion with one another in Christ does not produce uniformity. It rather generates diversity. In becoming one with Christ and with all creation in him, each individual attains optimum development of his/her unique personhood.

Thus, these questions arise for prospective celibates: Do I accept others as they are and welcome diversity in communal life? Or do I want everyone to fit into the same mold?

4) *A Sense of Mission*

Christian community participates in the Trinity's creative and recapitulating activity. As the Father and the Son send forth their Spirit to enable us to participate in the Trinity, so God sends forth each Christian to collaborate in the Spirit's work of recapitulating all in Christ.

A further sign then of a celibate vocation is a sense of mission, an awareness of being sent forth to others in the name of Jesus.[2] God endows every person with a mission. So, this sign is not an exclusive prerogative of celibacy. However, if God is calling a person to a celibate lifestyle, a sense of mission will indeed be present.

The word "mission" signifies a calling to go forth and to witness Christ within his Church and to the world. The term "ministry" designates that which God gives us to do once we

[2]See *Contemplation,* 133–140.

are sent forth. Ministry thus refers to a specific aspect of mission. Over a period of time, a person's mission can include a number of different ministries.

Jesus acknowledges his consciousness of mission:

> I am sent forth by the living Father (John 6:57);
>
> I know the Father because he has sent me forth (John 7:29);
>
> Not that I came because I chose to come;
> no, I was sent forth by the Father (John 8:42).

Jesus in turn entrusts his disciples with the task of continuing his mission:

> As the Father has sent me forth,
> so I also send you (John 20:21; 17:18).

Two New Testament verbs nuance the notion of mission: *pémpo* (to send) and *apostéllo* (to send forth). While the two can be used interchangeably, *pémpo* frequently stresses the action of sending, as in:

> If I leave,
> I will send the Holy Spirit to you (John 16:7).

Apostéllo, on the other hand, accentuates the one doing the sending, as well as the mission to be accomplished:

> There was a man sent forth from God,
> whose name was John (John 1:6);
>
> As you, Father, have sent me forth into the world,
> so do I send them forth into the world (John 17:18).

In biblical thought, the sender and the person sent are one. The sender brings him/herself to others in and through the person missioned. Thus, the Father manifests himself to his people in and through Jesus whom he missions:

> Whoever believes in me
> believes . . . in the one who sent me.
> And whoever sees me,
> sees the one who sent me (John 12:44-45).

Jesus also reveals himself in and through those whom he commissions in his name. So intimate is this union between Christ and those sent that he affirms:

> Whoever welcomes the one I send
> welcomes me.
> And whoever welcomes me
> welcomes the one who sent me (John 13:20).

Mission thus implies outward movement, a thrust forward in such a way that the sender and the one sent go forth together. Jesus says of the Father: "The one who sent me is with me" (John 8:29). After commissioning his disciples to go out and to evangelize all nations, Jesus promises: "I am with you always; yes, even to the end of time" (Matt 28:20).

Apostéllo denotes not only the activity of sending, but also the notion of sending *forth*. Love impels the one sent, while remaining in Father, Son and Spirit, toward service to God's people. That person experiences an impulse to do something particular for God, so that Christ can bring himself more fully to the world. That impetus comes from Jesus himself:

> From Christ the whole body . . . builds itself up in love,
> as each part does its work (Eph 4:16).

Yet, being sent forth does not consist only in an outward movement. While going out, the person's activity has also a quality of interiorization. Mission encompasses both centrifugal and centripetal energies. The Christian's communion in solitude of heart with Jesus progresses even in the activity of going forth. Moreover, because those to whom the person is sent are also sent by God to that individual, the mission becomes a providential instrument of spiritual growth for the one sent. A threefold movement is thus generated: in sending me to you, Christ sends you to me, in such a way that both of us are united more deeply in him.

To be sent forth is to be pilgrim. In the biblical notion of mission, we see in microcosm the process of coming from the Father and of returning to him with Jesus in the Spirit.

Therefore, prospective celibates need to discern whether they possess a sense of mission. Moreover, they need to examine whether they experience being sent forth as an essential dimension of their personal relationship with Jesus. Absence of a sense of mission or an inability to situate mission in the context of a relationship with the Lord can be counterindicative of a calling to the celibate life.

CHAPTER 17

Celibate Love

The phrase "celibate love" says diverse things to different people. It can have also a variety of meanings for the same person, depending on the relationships at issue. By celibate love, we understand a profound experience of human affection between a man and a woman or between two people of the same sex in which at least one of them is a celibate at heart.

No one person or succession of amorous relationships can exhaust the infinite capacity of the human heart to love and to be loved. Therefore, it is not unusual for a married man or woman to experience an exciting fondness, warmth or tenderness for someone other than his/her spouse. The affection can even reach the intensity of being-in-love. A wedded person's ability to integrate this experience can spell the difference between marital recommitment and marital breakup.

By the same token, it is not unusual for celibates at heart to experience profound love for—perhaps even being-in-love with—someone other than the Lord. When that occurs, many celibates undergo a radical reevaluation of their vocational lifestyle. They ask: How truly celibate am I? What might God be revealing to me through this unsought relationship? Needless to say, the manner in which celibates integrate this love into their life affects deeply their affective and spiritual maturation.

When celibates by circumstance become involved in a true love relationship, the affective interaction tends to catapult them into mature vocational consciousness: be it an awareness of a calling to celibacy at heart, marriage or singlehood.

Human language and conventional thought patterns remain sorely limited when it comes to expressing the mystery of interpersonal affection. In the context of celibate love, those limits are immeasurably compounded. Nonetheless, in recent years a growing number of competent people have addressed the issue of celibate love from various perspectives: emotional, psychosexual, developmental, theological, ascetical, etc. Our presentation highlights certain principles of vocational discernment regarding celibate love which do not always receive sufficient emphasis.

In this chapter we focus on three principles of discernment which pertain to the inner dynamics of celibate love: It is a gift from God. It is a unique kind of love. It entails transformation and purification.

A. Love as Divine Gift

Every true love is a gift from God. As divine gift, love is innately directed toward the progressive spiritualization of the recipient. Human love is a created participation in the inner life of God who is Love (1 John 4:8, 16).

The person whom the Lord gifts with love for another cannot not love him/her. That person may try to deny or to refuse the gift. Yet, if God has ignited the flame, the fire will persist. The individual can choose not to enter an intimate relationship with the loved one. But, if the Lord is its source, the affective impetus remains.

God bestows some gifts so that the recipients can sacrifice them to God. God endows recipients with other gifts to use and to develop also for God. Conferring upon a celibate a special love for another human being entails both sacrificing the gift and using it. Both aspects are operative as the two persons seek to express their love in accord with their respective vocations.

Many celibates by circumstance who are in reality marriageable are prone to set themselves up for amorous pursuits. Whether they admit it or not, they tend toward romantic intimacy. Celibates at heart, on the other hand, do not deliberately seek amorous relationships. Even though celibates at heart are not immune from infatuation or affective immaturities, they do not date or court. They do not spend their leisure in singles or gay bars. They do not look for erotic stimulation through reading or talking, from music or dance, in movies or videos. Clearly, celibates at heart undergo normal affective attractions, but in these warm and tender regards they experience themselves as unmarriageable by vocation. No matter how strong the attraction, they are nonetheless at home and at peace being unmarriageable. Celibates at heart remain open to the possibility of a celibate love because God may wish to bestow it. At the same time they do not search for it because to do so would be unfaithful to their calling.

True love for a spouse is essential to a vocation to marriage. Affective involvement with another person is not a requirement for a celibate vocation. Celibate love is a gift freely given, within a basic calling. Some receive it, others do not. That gift does not proceed directly from the celibate's unmarriageable status. Nor is it in spite of or outside his/her celibacy. If both the celibacy and the celibate love are from God, they are innately compatible. The challenge for the celibate is to integrate this gift with his/her basic vocational lifestyle.

Jesus invites all of us—married, celibate, single—to love the Lord with all our heart, mind and strength (Mark 12:28-31). That invitation does not imply emptying ourselves of our human affections and then substituting God in their place. Rather, Christ's invitation calls us to come to him with all our specific loves, regardless of their degree of maturity, so that he can purify and transform them.[1]

Jesus invites us not only to love our neighbor as ourselves (Mark 12:31), but also to love one another as he himself loves us (John 15:12), which is as the Father loves him (John 15:9). That invitation has special application to the mystery of celibate love. Ultimately then, God's gift enables the celibate to love the other person with God's own love—that is, in a manner which participates in the Father's love for the Son and the Son's love for us. That quality of loving may be possible only after many years of struggle or at the end of one's life. Nonetheless, that quality of loving remains the ideal of not only celibate love, but also every human love.

[1]See *O Blessed Night,* 176; *Receptivity,* 119.

The prayer of Jesus "that all may be one" (John 17:21) also has particular application to the gift of celibate love. Jesus wills the affective interchange between the celibate and the other person, as well as between the two of them and himself. Gifting them with celibate love, Christ enables them to become "one" in a spiritual friendship and "one" in him. That loving interchange participates in the inner life of the Trinity:

> Father, may they be one in us
> as you are in me and as I am in you (John 17:21).

All true love participates in divine *agápe,* which is Father, Son and Spirit loving each other in us. Love is then not only gift *from* God, but also gift *of* God as God (1 John 4:8, 16). By means of celibate love, Jesus within one person loves Jesus in the other so that there is but "one Christ loving himself."[2]

Whatever the basic vocational lifestyles of the two persons involved, any gift of loving communion is a means through which God's love is active in the world:

> With me in them and you, Father, in me,
> may they be so completely one
> that the world will realize that it was you who sent me
> and that I love them as much as you love me (John 17:23).

Love between two people may be publicly recognized and sacramentalized as in the case of matrimony. It may be private and known only to a few. In some instances, the gift may remain hidden in God, perceived only by the two persons who receive it. Whatever the case, mutual love is an instrument through which the Lord's compassion penetrates the world and a means through which two persons experience and witness divine *agápe.*

As gift, celibate love is usually bestowed in the raw and received into vessels of clay. The love itself is fragile. It requires careful and responsible nurturing. Its recipients, all too subject to human frailty, have the potential to abuse it or to express it in ways that God does not intend.

[2]St. Augustine, *The First Letter of John 5:13* (*PL,* 35:2055).

B. The Nature and the Purpose of Celibate Love

Love has many modalities. Forms of affective interaction include parent and child, brother and sister, friend and friend, husband and wife. There is love of friendship (*phílos*), love of lovers (*éros*) and love of God (*agápe*). Sometimes all three modes are present in a single act of loving. At other times and for a variety of reasons they are differentiated. Furthermore, it is one thing to simply love a person and quite another to be-in-love with him/her.

When a celibate experiences love for another human being, it is important to discern the nature and the purpose of the gift. What is it that God entrusts, and why does God bestow it?

Celibate love is for most people a modality of the love of friendship. God desires celibate love to be a matrix of transformation and purification for each of the persons involved. God wishes also the love itself to be transformed and purified.

It is possible for a celibate to be-in-love with another person. Celibate being-in-love is exceptional mainly for three reasons: 1) God rarely endows this gift on two persons not called also to marriage. 2) To receive this gift and yet remain celibate for the sake of Jesus and the gospel requires extraordinary maturity and grace. 3) A celibate does not ordinarily have in relation to the loved one the long-term proximity necessary for being-in-love to develop and to mature.

Life is seldom unambiguous or ideal. Even two mature persons may find it difficult, especially at the outset, to identify where their affective relationship is heading. While they live it out within the context of a Christocentric commitment, some recipients experience celibate love as anything but platonic. Particularly at the beginning it may seem that erotic desire will consume them. Yet, celibates neither repress that desire nor act upon it. Rather, they learn to sublimate it.

Imbalances in a celibate's life give rise to turmoil and ambivalence regarding the loved one. The presence of any of the following conditions makes discernment of a particular relationship intricate and complex:

> 1) The celibate has not yet successfully passed through the preadolescent or the adolescent phases of psychosexual development.

2) The celibate is going through midlife crisis.

3) The celibate is struggling with both adolescent and midlife issues of psychosexual development.

4) A psychological dysfunctionality is operative in the celibate's life.

5) Difficulties with ministry, community or family of origin leave the celibate craving affection and affirmation.

Because of the heightened vulnerability or the immaturity inherent in the above situations, the celibate is susceptible to being swept off his/her feet. In the confusion and hurt, s/he is all too prone to mistake infatuation or momentary relief for love.

A celibate man who has not sufficiently integrated qualities generally considered as feminine or a celibate woman who has not adequately integrated qualities commonly designated as masculine will experience havoc in affective relationships. That man tends to project his *anima* onto specific women. That woman is apt to project her *animus* onto certain men. In both cases, they easily misinterpret as love the intense emotional reactions that ensue. As long as the projections last, what the man or the woman loves is a reflection in another of certain potential qualities within him/herself. Amid such entanglement, it becomes difficult, if not impossible, to see another person as s/he is. Resolution of this type of projection is necessary before a man or a woman can discern whether s/he truly loves another.

Whatever the intensity of friendship—casual, good, close, very special, inseparable, beloved—imbalances in the celibate's life can trigger strong impulses to express love inappropriately. Imbalances give rise also to distressing questions about basic vocational lifestyle.

C. The Transformation of Celibate Love

This side of the resurrection, any celibate love relationship is progressing from immaturity to maturity, from scatteredness to wholeness, from self-gratification to communion of spirits. The relationship passes through various thresholds and stages of development. Each stage of growth has its own crises and challenges. A spiritual director encounters a celibate at a specific point along the way. God calls the director to help the directee to discern the progress of the relationship, to focus on the pertinent issues and to ask the correct questions.

Celibate love is a precious gift. It is also a dark night. Celibate love exerts both transforming and purifying influences upon its recipients. In being brought to optimum union in Christ Jesus, two persons undergo a dying to self and to each other. True love detaches as it unites, wounds as it causes delight.[3]

Two characteristics of celibate love exert marked influence on the transformative process: nonexclusivity and the inevitability of eventual separation.

1) *Nonexclusivity*

Celibate love does not create a closed world for two. It is not based on jealousy or possessiveness. It does not exclude anyone or anything. On the contrary, while it retains all the uniqueness of a particular affection, celibate love tends toward all-embraciveness. It welcomes the diverse influences of life. It freely interacts with other loves. The more a celibate love approximates *agápe,* the more cosmic it becomes.

The nonexclusivity of celibate love expresses itself in three ways: a) However intense both the affection and the turmoil, the prime focus of the celibate remains the person of Jesus. Love for Christ incorporates and integrates all other loves into itself. b) Celibate love for an individual does not exclude other loves of similar nature and expression. Thus, unlike in marriage, the uniqueness of the love does not imply exclusivity. Therefore, c) a celibate's love for a person does not exclude either of them from forming friendships and associations with others at the same time or in the future.

2) *Eventual Separation*

Those whom God brings together spiritually in celibate love, God eventually separates in terms of physical proximity. Two persons' availability for interaction diminishes significantly as their lives and ministries evolve. Inevitably, the two have to

[3]See *O Blessed Night,* 63–68, 158–163; *Receptivity,* 26–31.

undergo the grieving process implicit in separation. Yet, in going their separate ways they reach the fullness which God intends for their love.

In the resurrection, God transforms celibate love and celibacy itself. Yet, already in this pilgrim existence, celibate love not only transforms but also is being transformed. Something of the initial experience of the love passes away, and something continues to develop. With the passage of time, both the quality and the expression of the love differ greatly from the earlier stages of the affection. As God strips away self-deception and illusion, the celibate may find the love to be entirely other than initially imagined.

Each mode of love undergoes its own evolution towards optimum spiritualization. Although celibate love changes, to the degree that it participates in *agápe* something of its deepest core endures purified and transformed. Like all true love, celibate love is for now and forever.

CHAPTER 18

The Expression of Celibate Love

The human spirit is enfleshed. Communion between human spirits transpires ordinarily through some form of physical contact. Simply put: Our "soul" needs a body. That truth underlies the celebration of the Christian sacraments. We encounter the mystery of God's transforming love in bread, wine, oil, water, gestures, words, etc. Those symbols become meeting points of the Holy Spirit and our spirit. Sacramental encounter expresses our faith, hope and love as it facilitates their intensification.

In this life, affective encounter between two people usually requires some corporeal interaction. Love spontaneously seeks to express itself. Human love needs to be embodied in words, symbols or actions. Tangible expressions of love in turn facilitate the spiritualization of a relationship.

Appropriate ways of expressing affection differ radically for celibate, engaged, married and single persons. Even within a given relationship the expression of love is constantly changing. It varies as the love itself matures. It shifts also as each person's vocational consciousness evolves.

A. Appropriate Interaction

In a celibate love relationship—whether heterosexual or homosexual—the following question inevitably arises: What is an appropriate expression of this love?

As long as the affection remains within the mode of a good or a close friendship, the manner of expressing it is relatively simple to discern. The two persons care for each other and express their affection like ordinary good or close friends do, always acknowledging that at least one of them is celibate.

The situation, however, becomes intricate when the affection contains overtones of romantic love or deep emotional involvement. These circumstances give rise to much anxiety and ambiguity. Many celibates in this context instinctively ask: "If I am celibate at heart yet feel drawn to such intimacy with this person, how honest is my commitment to God? How can I be so affectively attracted to a human being and remain Christ-centered? Do I truly love either one? How can I love both?"

Those are indeed agonizing questions. Moreover, since love is so qualitative and ineffable, clear-cut answers are virtually impossible. What seems contradictory to the human mind may not be so from the Lord's perspective. God does gift some celibates with a very special love for another person. Since the Lord does not bestow contradictory gifts, these celibates can find a way to integrate the affective relationship with their consecration.

In celibate love there is no pat answer to the issue of appropriate expression. Each affection is unique and uncharted. That is a first principle of discernment. The second flows from it: Each celibate love has to discover its own way. Discerning that way begins with formulating the correct question.

1) *An Incorrect Question*

Many people struggling with the issue of celibate love sooner or later ask: "How far can I go?" That is an incorrect question. Any direct answer to it is bound to be deficient and misleading.

In most instances, "How far can I go?" reflects a legalistic or static mind-set. It focuses almost exclusively on physical acts and anatomy. "How far can I go?" smacks of reliance on external authority for clear-cut boundaries, instead of trusting personal responsibility and a sense of vocation. Frequently, what underlies the question is a dichotomy between body and soul, matter and spirit, natural and "supernatural." The celibate may have not yet succeeded in reconciling the sexual and the transcendent dimensions of personal interaction. And, even if no fundamental dichotomy exists, the question contains considerable narcissistic inference. "How far can I go?"

implies in effect: "How far can I gratify my appetites, my desires, my self?"

To pose the question more accurately, we take a relational and developmental approach—one which appreciates human attitudes and actions in light of their effects on the loved one and on the dynamics of the relationship.

2) *The Crucial Question*

The appropriate inquiry—indeed, the critical question—is: How much interaction is necessary in the celibate love relationship to attain an optimum of spirit?[1]

The starting point, the goal and the principle animating every gift of love is *optimum of spirit*. The key spiritualizing force in the universe is God's *agápe*. To the extent that a love participates in divine love it is directed toward spiritualization. The word "optimum" highlights the most qualitative mode of being. It is used instead of "maximum" which implies quantity. Two persons involved in a celibate love relationship are called not to a mediocre or compromising affection, but to the most qualitative and hence spiritualizing mode of loving possible. Thus, they seek to let their love become all that God desires it to be.

To move in the direction of optimum spiritualization, some *interaction* between the two persons is necessary. Depending on many factors—vocational lifestyle being paramount—that interaction entails varying degrees of sexual, emotional, physical and spiritual encounters.

We distinguish "sexual encounter" from "genital encounter." Sexual encounter for a mature person suggests being at home with one's sexuality, free from compulsive acting-out and impulsive repression. Sexual encounter for a mature individual implies being comfortable with one's sexuality, able to deal constructively with sexual attraction and sexual arousal.

[1]See Pierre Teilhard de Chardin, "The Evolution of Chastity," *Toward the Future* (New York: Harcourt, 1973) 60–87; *O Blessed Night*, 158–163, 171–177; *Receptivity*, 44–48, 109–114. Teilhard's phrase in French is "*Combien du corps, pour un optimum d'esprit?*" (ibid., 79). Literally translated, it reads: "How much body for an optimum of spirit?" Teilhard uses the term "body," however, in the Pauline sense of the whole person but with accent on the tangible observable dimensions of that person.

In a heterosexual relationship, sexual encounter means a woman experiencing herself as woman in the eyes of a man and a man experiencing himself as man in the eyes of a woman. In a homosexual relationship, sexual encounter connotes a woman experiencing herself as a sexual being in the eyes of a woman and a man experiencing himself as a sexual being in the eyes of a man. Other forms of sexual encounter also exist: for instance, a child's discovery of sexual identity through identification with the parent of the same sex. Sexual encounter is a healthy and necessary part of human psychosexual development. In marriage genital encounter is a particularly meaningful way of celebrating sexual encounter. In inappropriate contexts, genital encounter can militate against and even destroy the significance of sexual encounter.

By "emotional encounter" we understand appropriate expressions of feelings for each other by means of words, actions or silence.

By "physical encounter" we call attention to proximity. Physical encounter involves activities such as working together or sharing one another's company.

By "spiritual encounter" we mean that each one consciously supports the other on his/her unique journey with Christ to the Father through the Spirit.

Yet, the crux of the question remains: *How much* interaction *is necessary in the relationship?* The phrase "optimum of spirit" suggests quality. The phrase "how much" bespeaks quantity. While quality and quantity pertain to different realms, they interrelate throughout this mortal existence. For some persons, it takes a lot of interaction to direct their love toward spirit. For other people, a minimum of interaction catapults their love in the direction of optimum spirit. Too much interaction can suffocate spirit. Too little interaction can leave spirit frustrated. Furthermore, interaction can increase, decrease or remain practically the same as celibate love matures. There are no predictable patterns. A specific "how much" cannot be fixed *a priori* or applied universally. "How much interaction" depends on the internal demands of each love in view of the spiritualization to which God destines it. Each celibate love has to be discerned on its own merits, and that discernment must remain ongoing.

The particular optimum of spirit to which God calls two people determines the appropriate amount of interaction. Love imparts its own wisdom. To determine how much interaction, the celibate needs to listen to the wisdom flowing from that love. In this respect, the advice of the author of the *Cloud of Unknowing* is applicable:

> If you wish to be off quickly and unerringly on your spiritual journey, one thing suffices and nothing more: God alive in your mind and active in your heart, gently arousing you to everlasting love. . . . This very love you experience tells you unerringly when to speak and when to be silent. It will guide you discreetly and without error in everything. It will enlighten you in secret with great and surpassing discretion, teaching you when to begin and when to leave off. . . . This love will immediately take the initiative and gently prod you [to know and to do whatever is necessary].[2]

Qoheleth offers similar advice in his understanding of a time, a place and an intensity for everything, including affective relating. Thus, there is:

> A time for mourning,
> and a time for dancing . . .
> A time for embracing,
> and a time to refrain from embracing . . .
> A time for remaining silent,
> and a time for speaking.
> A time for loving,
> and a time for [letting go] (Eccl 3:4-8).

With regard to celibate love, the celibate tests his/her discernment by discussing the progress of the relationship with the loved one as well as with a spiritual director, confessor, confidant or friend. Dialogue with these people is important lest the celibate fall into self-deception and illusion. It takes much honesty, common sense, challenge and flexibility to work through the intricacies of celibate love.

3) *Communion in Love Without a Formal Covenant*

In some celibate love relationships, this question arises: Is it appropriate for the two persons to express their mutual af-

[2] "A Pistle of Discrecioun of Stirings," *Contemplative Review* 10 (1, 1977) 17–18.

fection in a formal, though private, bond or covenant? In our pastoral experience we have yet to encounter an instance in which God seemed to be eliciting such a step. In the cases that have come to our attention where two persons desired to make or actually formalized such a bond or covenant, the following dispositions have prevailed. In some situations the two became more "married" than celibate. In other cases the twosome consisted of a single person wanting marriage and the other—either celibate at heart or by circumstance—not wishing formal marriage. In a few instances the two entered into a quasi-domestic partnership.

In our view celibate love expressed in a formal covenant seems incongruous with authentic celibacy. Furthermore, such a bond appears incompatible with the nonexclusive character of celibate love. If two people deem such covenanting necessary, perhaps their love is other than celibate.

Each love spontaneously establishes its own spiritual bond. Covenanting between a celibate and another person remains within that spiritual realm and does not need formal definition or explicitness.

B. The Celibate Relationship Itself

Whenever a celibate enters into an affective relationship, whether heterosexual or homosexual, the other person is either celibate, married or single. Each of these three possibilities presents its own complex of issues:

1) *Between Two Authentic Celibates*

When two celibates at heart love one another, they encounter each other out of their celibate consecration. Thus, they meet on relatively equal footing. Each possesses a psychosexual history with its specific strengths and weaknesses. Yet, the two persons know where they stand in terms of basic vocational lifestyle and commitment. They speak the same language and have fundamentally the same optimum of spirit as their goal. Emotional upheaval may still occur. Considerable ambiguity and struggle may lie ahead. Nonetheless, they share a common sense of direction in their relationship.

2) *Between a Celibate and a Married Person*

When a celibate and a married person experience love, that situation can pose special problems. For one thing, the married person has a history of genital expression of love. The celibate supposedly does not.

The affective relationship of the married person with his/her spouse is of paramount importance. Are they happily married or on the verge of breakup? Is their union vibrant or virtually nonexistent? Does the person find relative fulfillment in the marriage, or is s/he looking for something basic which that relationship lacks? Existence of a sense of vocation with regard to the marriage goes a long way toward directing the relationships with both the spouse and the celibate toward an optimum of spirit.

The maturity of the celibate's vocational awareness is of equal gravity. Is s/he celibate at heart and thus committed to Jesus out of a sense of vocation. Or is s/he in reality celibate by circumstance. If the latter is the case, the person could be in effect single and unconsciously looking for a spouse.

A celibate and a married person encounter each other affectively out of very different lifestyles and life histories. Therefore, their interaction has to remain generally more restrained than between two celibates at heart. That restraint is necessary if they are to direct their love toward an optimum of spirit.

3) *Between a Celibate and a Single Person*

A particularly difficult situation occurs when a celibate and a single person find themselves emotionally involved. In the case of a celibate at heart and a person married out of a sense of vocation, both are formally consecrated to someone and remain, existentially speaking, unmarriageable. Most single men and women are marriageable.

The celibate and the single person approach each other not only out of radically different lifestyles but also from profoundly diverse mind-sets and emotional expectations. On a motivational level the celibate could be merely dining out with a special friend, while the single person could actually be dating the celibate. Rarely do the two have the same suppositions behind affective language or the same interpretation of one another's nonverbal communication. Moreover, each of them has vastly differing affective needs.

For all practical purposes many celibates by circumstance or individuals married for reasons other than a sense of calling can be considered single persons in the context of vocational discernment.

C. Celibates by Circumstance Who Discern a Calling to Marriage

The love of a celibate at heart for another person can for a while occasion a vocational crisis. When it does so, the love becomes in the long run instrumental in the growth of the celibate's vocational consciousness and commitment to God through celibacy.

In the case of celibates by circumstance, a special love for another person inevitably causes a vocational crisis. That crisis leads either to the realization of a calling to celibacy at heart or to the acknowledgement of not being called at all to celibacy. Affective involvement with another person forces celibates by circumstance to confront the question of their true vocational lifestyle. The experience of love catapults them to a new plateau of self-knowledge. They thus receive further insight into their personal identity and increased awareness of what they really desire. That discovery contributes significantly to the maturation of their vocational consciousness and to the development of the freedom to respond accordingly.

In the context of a heterosexual relationship, a celibate by circumstance who loves another and discerns a calling to marriage may find him/herself in one of these situations: 1) Assuming that the desire for conjugal life is mutual, the two persons decide to marry. Or 2) the celibate finds that despite his/her yearning to marry, the loved one is unable or unwilling to wed.

When marriage does not occur, several directions are open to the celibate by circumstance:

> 1) S/he may decide to continue living a kind of celibate life for the time being, since the person whom s/he desires to marry is unavailable. If the celibate by circum-

stance is indeed aware of a calling to marriage, persistence in celibacy lacks some degree of authenticity. All God may have intended from that relationship was to bring the celibate by circumstance to a consciousness of his/her basic calling. The individual whom God intends him/her to wed may come along only later.

2) The celibate by circumstance chooses to enter an active genital relationship with the other person. That decision radically alters the situation. S/he is no longer living celibately in any sense.

3) The celibate by circumstance takes on a secret pseudo-marriage or quasi-domestic partnership with someone real or imagined. Needless to say, a duality of this nature can wreak havoc in an individual's life.

4) The celibate by circumstance opts to live as celibate a life as possible until death, trusting in God to provide the necessary grace. Ordinarily, that option requires nothing less than heroic virtue.

5) The celibate by circumstance passes the threshold—even if only minimally so—of personal consecration. That is to say: "I would prefer to marry. But that is not possible. Nonetheless, I interpret this impossibility as providential. Therefore, I choose celibacy for Christ and the gospel out of a vague sense that God seems to be calling me to it."

In the context of a homosexual relationship, when a celibate by circumstance experiences not only intense love for a person but also enters into a genital relationship with the other, the celibate status changes radically. In effect, what has happened is cessation of a celibate lifestyle and commencement of an active homosexual lifestyle. This person is no longer celibate in any sense.

In a heterosexual context, when a celibate by circumstance realizes through a love relationship that s/he is not called to celibacy, the usual course is to seek release from the celibate commitment in order to freely pursue the relationship. In a homosexual context, when a celibate by circumstance realizes through a love relationship that s/he is not called to celibacy, the person can be sorely tempted to retain the external trappings of celibacy. For some people, that temptation is virtually irresistible. "Celibacy" then constitutes a socially acceptable cover for what has become an active homosexual lifestyle.

Knowingly and willingly living the pretext of celibacy would be not only hypocritical for a person—whether heterosexual or homosexual—but also damaging to the institution to which that individual belongs.

CHAPTER 19

Pastoral Observations

Throughout our discussion of celibacy as a basic Christian lifestyle we have used a relational model of approach. In this paradigm, the core of celibacy consists of a twofold dynamic: 1) Jesus calling forth within a person a celibate relatedness to himself; 2) then, in Christ, the celibate relating to him/herself, other people and all creation. This relational model differs from behavioral and ministerial models which define celibacy primarily vis-á-vis sexuality and ministry.

We now conclude these chapters on the celibate life with a brief synthesis of the principles for discernment and a few further suggestions for pastoral implementation.

A. Commitment in Faith

In describing a calling to the celibate life, we identified the following principles of discernment as indicative of mature vocational consciousness.

> 1) Celibacy for the sake of Jesus and the Gospel is a gift to an individual and a gift to God's people. A celibate commitment emerges from a particular experience of being loved by Christ and of loving him in response. In that loving interchange, the person experiences at some point a specific vocational imperative: an existential inability to become other than celibate.
>
> 2) Celibacy entails self-commitment to the person of Jesus. A celibate lifestyle, therefore, flows from and redounds to an all-embracing relationship with Christ, as well as with the Father and the Spirit. Some people, how-

ever, make a celibate commitment for other reasons. Inadequate motives include:

- celibacy principally for the sake of availability for ministry;
- celibacy primarily as a condition for membership in a religious institute;
- celibacy viewed as offering to everyone a more advantageous relationship than does marriage or singlehood;
- celibacy assumed out of conformity to the expectations of significant persons in one's life.

Other situations also can be counterindicative of a Christocentric focus in commitment. These include: lack of sufficient self-identity, externalism in prayer, negative attitudes toward marriage and inordinate desire for security.

3) The celibate life is holistically oriented. Loving communion with the indwelling Trinity integrates all aspects of a celibate's life. Many forms of prayer, especially solitary prayer, serve to deepen a celibate commitment. A celibate at heart experiences the need to go apart on a regular basis from his/her usual concerns and activities in order to be alone with Jesus. In interpersonal relationships, the celibate practices a form of chastity expressive of his/her unique relationship with Christ.

4) A calling to be celibate is also a vocation to be solitary. The realization of radical aloneness develops especially through the celibate's involvement with creation and his/her voluntary foregoing of marriage and family life. As solitary, the celibate is called to continuous loving communion with the indwelling Father, Son and Spirit as well as with all creation in God.

5) The solitary person who is celibate for the sake of Jesus and the Gospel stands in special relationship to Christian community. The celibate's solitude is the foundation of his/her union with other persons in God. Like love, which is its basis, solitude unites and differentiates. Authentic solitude generates indepth communion with others. In community, the celibate values and fosters the

uniqueness of each member. Thus, community thrives on diversity. The celibate has also a sense of being sent by Jesus to witness within the Church and to the world. For many celibates, this witness entails an ecclesial ministry.

6) The question of celibate love can arise in the context of discernment of a possible calling to the celibate life.

> a) Celibate love is a gift from God. If both the celibate calling and the love are from the Lord, they are integrable. Celibate love is ordinarily a modality of the love of friendship (*phílos*). In some instances, however, it consists of a deep personal love (*agápe*) or even being-in-love with another person. Whatever the modality of celibate love, it undergoes transformation and purification as it unites and detaches the two persons.
>
> b) The crucial question in discerning a possible celibate love relationship is this: How much interaction is necessary between the two persons in order to attain an optimum of spirit? Whether the celibate is involved affectively with another celibate, a married or a single person has considerable bearing on the dynamics of the relationship. Celibate love has to be responsibly nurtured.
>
> c) For a celibate at heart, the gift of a special love for another person ultimately intensifies celibate commitment. The tension and the searching which accompany this gift occur in the context of mature vocational consciousness and commitment. Thus, if a vocational crisis results from the relationship, it cannot but strengthen a celibate's resolve.
>
> d) For many celibates by circumstance, the experience of human love forces them to confront the question of their true vocational lifestyle. Some are led into celibacy at heart, others come to recognize that marriage or singlehood is their calling.

The above principles of discernment vary in intensity from one person to another. Even within an individual's experience, some of those signs may be faintly present, while others are clearly manifest. At any point in a person's spiritual journey, certain principles may be more accentuated than others. Often, some doubt and much struggle arise from the fact that certain immaturities and possible counterindications exist along with perceptible positive signs.

Even after careful deliberation on the principles of discernment for a possible vocation to celibacy, commitment to Jesus and the Gospel through a celibate lifestyle is made in faith:

- faith in God and in oneself;
- faith tried in the crucible of time and experience;
- faith seeking understanding and attested by signs;
- faith which remains dark and risk-filled yet impelling;
- faith which prompts the heart to recognize reasons that reason cannot fathom;
- faith impelling the pilgrim to affirm his/her existential inability to become other than celibate.

B. Useful Pastoral Distinctions

In relation to the principles of discernment which we explored in these chapters on celibate life, we highlight certain distinctions which may be useful to aspirants, spiritual directors, formation teams and seminary personnel:

1) *Concerning a Priest Member of a Religious Institute*

In the case of a person aspiring to become both a member of a religious congregation and an ordained presbyter, there are at least three distinct vocations and four discernments to be considered:

- first, the vocational issue of whether the individual has a calling to celibacy as a basic Christian lifestyle;
- second, the vocational issue of the religious life. This entails two discernments:

  a) the possible calling to the religious life in general, since not all celibates are called also to be religious;

  b) the possible calling to a specific religious community, since there are many;

- third, the vocational issue of a calling to the presbyterate as a specific order and ministry within the Church. (See the *Appendix*.)

Because all four discernments often go on simultaneously, the above sequence represents a logical order rather than a chronological order. The three vocational focuses and the four discernments intricately interrelate among themselves and converge within the same individual. Nonetheless, at some point the aspirant must address each of them on its own merits. For every vocation possesses its own principles of discernment and manifests its own signs of authenticity.

2) *Concerning a Religious Brother or Sister*

In the case of religious brothers and sisters, there are also at least three distinct vocations and four discernments to consider:

- first, the vocational issue of a calling to celibacy;
- second, the vocational issue of the religious life. This entails two discernments:
  - a) the calling to the religious life in general;
  - b) the calling to a specific religious community;
- third, the vocational issue of a calling to a ministry within the charism of that institute.

3) *Concerning a Diocesan Priest*

Given current legislation in the Roman Catholic Church regarding clerical celibacy, at least two distinct vocations require discernment in the case of a person seeking to serve as a diocesan priest:

- first, the vocational issue of a personal calling to celibacy as a basic lifestyle, independent of a possible calling to the presbyterate;
- second, the vocational issue of a calling to presbyteral ministry within the Church.

The first is a calling to a vocational "how": how the person is to become transformed in God. The second is a calling to a vocational "what": what the person is sent forth to do for God and God's people. (See the *Appendix*.) Assuming that the above two discernments are positive, further discernment is required to determine to which expression of presbyteral ministry God is calling the priest in question.

4) *Concerning a Deacon*

Given current canonical legislation in the Roman Catholic Church regarding transitional and permanent deacons, there are at least two distinct vocations to be discerned:

- first, the vocational issue of a calling to a basic Christian lifestyle: married, celibate or single. Before receiving ordination, a candidate needs to have attained mature vocational consciousness regarding one of those lifestyles.
- second, if the person is not going on to the presbyterate, the vocational issue of a calling to the permanent diaconate as a distinct ecclesial order and office. (See the *Appendix*.)

For someone seeking presbyteral ordination, the transitional diaconate does not seem to be a distinct vocational issue, but rather a step in view of the next order.

5) *Concerning a Bishop*

One can dispute theologically the difference between the order of presbyter and the order of bishop. Nonetheless, in terms of ecclesial practice considerable difference exists. (See the *Appendix*.) Thus, we perceive the calling of a presbyter to episcopal ordination as a distinct vocational issue.

We presuppose that prior to the discernment of a calling to episcopal ordination the prospective bishop has reached mature vocational consciousness of a calling to celibacy as the basic lifestyle. If not, due to current legislation on clerical celibacy in the Roman Catholic Church, the issue must be resolved before accepting the episcopate.

Regarding a calling to the episcopacy specifically as a distinct office within the Church, discernment focuses on its ministerial dimensions. Although a person could be ordained a bishop without passing through the diaconate and the presbyterate, that procedure is rare in Church history and would be almost unimaginable today.

C. A Pastoral Counsel

Whatever the actual situation, spiritual directors, formation teams, seminary personnel and all other duly interested parties must accustom themselves to taking all the time necessary for the Lord to unfold the various dimensions of a candidate's vocation. No one can assume that a person has a certain calling until God indicates that s/he does. Vocational lifestyles which entail a permanent commitment are ultimately experienced in terms of an existential inability to become otherwise. Until candidates are explicitly conscious of that vocational imperative, they are not ready to make a definitive commitment. To do so notwithstanding would be not only premature, but also presumptuous.

SINGLE LIFE

CHAPTER 20

Singlehood

There was a time when the prevailing attitude toward vocations ran something like this: The term "vocation" refers to priesthood or religious life, and both require celibacy. Marriage is for the masses of people unable to bridle their sexual urges. Single life is the predicament of those individuals who are without-a-vocation and left-out-of-marriage.

During the mid-twentieth century, that attitude began to change. Many people came to appreciate marriage as an authentic vocation. Some saw it as inferior to celibacy, but a true calling nonetheless. Others considered it on a par with celibacy. Singlehood, however, continued to be viewed as a non-vocation.

Today, even that attitude has changed. Not only are marriage and celibacy recognized as Christian vocational lifestyles in their own right, but so also singlehood. Now, few people would deny that God calls certain individuals to remain single.

Past attitudes toward singlehood reflected models which might be dubbed negational or nondescript. Those models perceived singlehood as a non-calling, a non-institution, a situation that one is left with when all else is eliminated. Single people were considered to exist in a sort of indefinable limbo betwixt and between marriage and celibacy. The model out of which our theology of singlehood flows is relational.

A. Single by Choice or by Circumstance

Each person starts off single. After some time most people marry, a few become celibate and an increasing number remain single. Among the latter, some are single by choice, others by circumstance. Those who are single by choice generally find their lifestyle challenging and invigorating. Those who are single by circumstance experience their singlehood as forced upon them in some way. Yet, with maturity and a sense of vocation, they can make a voluntary option for singlehood.

The phrase "single by circumstance" contains a myriad of nuances and covers a multitude of possibilities. Some people suffer irreversible infirmities which for them exclude matrimony. Many persons who are "married" or "celibate" for reasons other than a sense of vocation are in fact single. Some singles want desperately to marry, but cannot. Others do not want the responsibilities of wedded life, but neither do they desire the solitude of celibacy or the aloneness of singlehood. Still others happen to be single for the moment because they are on their way to marriage or celibacy.

B. Single for a While or for Life

In most instances a certain temporary quality characterizes choice of the single life, even when singlehood endures for a lifetime. Most people choose to remain single for now, for the time being. They are content to live singlehood day by day, since it does not require lifelong commitment. They are satisfied to let this lifestyle evolve on a wait-and-see basis according to God's design.

Some single persons later perceive vocations to marry or to become celibate. Others do not. The former are single for a while. The latter are single for life.

More and more people today remain single all their lives. At an early age, few of them expressly intend singlehood until death. At any moment along the way they experience relative fulfillment in their lifestyle. Then, later—usually in retrospect—they realize that singlehood had been God's calling from the outset.

A couple embarking upon marriage do so explicitly for as long as they both shall live. Even if canonically a person may vow or promise celibacy for a time, the inner dynamics of a celibate calling urge him/her toward lifelong commitment. The single life, on the other hand, stresses the present, without binding the future. Therefore, a significant sign that God may be calling a person to singlehood is the emergence in that individual of a positive sense of vocation toward the single life for now.

C. Motives for Choosing the Single Life

Why would a person opt to remain single, even when marriage or celibacy continues to be possible? There exist as many reasons as there are individual singles. In general, those motives fall under two large umbrellas: negative reasons and positive reasons.

The Don Juan or Doña Juana is single because s/he cannot sustain an affectionate relationship. Other people are single because nothing else works. They do not necessarily want to be single, but practically they have no choice. No one will marry them and celibacy does not attract them. Still others choose singlehood because they do not like the options open to them. They judge singlehood to be less threatening, less difficult, less exigent than other possibilities.

Notwithstanding the above negative motivations, positive reasons for a choice of the single life abound:

Some persons choose singlehood because of its suitability for a cause or a work. For instance, a person may decide to care for an infirm family member. The fulfillment of that responsibility could consume thirty or forty years of his/her life.

Other individuals choose singlehood for greater independence. They cherish their freedom. They enjoy the single life. They neither want nor require a marital partner or the responsibility of a family. On the contrary, these people need to be single for self-fulfillment. They experience meaningfulness in living alone—an aloneness which differs from the celibate's solitude and the egotist's isolation.[1]

Still others opt for singlehood for the sake of a career or a profession. These include committed teachers, dedicated social workers, devoted health care personnel, talented artists. These people may not have the slightest inclination toward religious life or any other form of celibate consecration. They

[1]See *Contemplation*, 97–99; *Spiritual Journey*, 62–71.

choose to remain single, and they choose to let that lifestyle take them where it will. It is not that their career or profession of itself excludes the possibility of marriage or celibacy, but rather that the single lifestyle best suits them as individuals. Friends or associates may claim: "They are married to their work." Maybe so, figuratively speaking. If such is the case, all the more reason for them to remain single!

We sometimes hear: "The right mate never came along." This does not necessarily imply that the single person was overly demanding of prospective spouses or negative toward marriage. It can be an accurate statement of fact. For it is better to choose to remain single than to marry the wrong person or to attempt marriage at any cost.

The presence of some negative motivation does not of itself exclude the possibility of a basically positive choice. God can use a person's shadowy side to set him/her in the right vocational direction. Moreover, some singles who begin in a negative frame of mind eventually change their attitude. They positively accept to remain single; even if given a viable alternative they might opt otherwise.

While there are specific reasons for each person's choice of the single life, the factor which underlies all others for mature Christians is God's calling. What God seems to will of them now and what they desire for themselves in terms of basic lifestyle is to remain single.

Therefore, when we speak of singlehood as a vocational lifestyle, we refer to singlehood positively chosen for the sake of Christ and the Gospel. Yet, not every positively chosen single life possesses that vocational quality. No one would be so naive as to assert that every swinging-single lifestyle is the result of a divine calling.

Some persons, however, seem to fall through the cracks of the three basic vocational lifestyles which we describe. For example, what certain people today term the single life appears in effect to be a informal expression of a veritable celibate lifestyle. For a variety of reasons, these individuals may not care to use the words "consecration," "celibacy" or even "Christ." Nonetheless, the inner thrust of the reality appears to be, by any other name, true celibacy. The converse also has merit. We find couples of so-called "singles"—whether homosexual or heterosexual—living together in deep bonds of love and mutual commitment. Society may not recognize these domestic partnerships as marriages, but the quality of their interchange transcends what some might call "living in sin."

D. Encounter with God Through the Single Life

Some persons encounter God in a unique manner in and through their single lifestyle just as authentically as others encounter God in and through marriage or celibacy.

God is with us always. Indeed, the Trinity abides within us twenty-four hours a day, seven days a week sustaining us in being, transforming us into the likeness of Christ and purging us of egocentricity. What then does it mean to encounter God when God is already more intimate to us then we are to ourselves?

The verb "to encounter" is derived from two Latin prepositions: *in* (toward, into) and *cóntra* (against). Its original meaning is to engage another. In reference to God to encounter is to experience the Lord's tender love and uncompromising desire for our transformation, which elicit our deepest love and commitment in response.

We encounter the Trinity *directly* (i.e., face to face in wordless, imageless loving communion) or *indirectly* (i.e., through/in the created). All three dimensions of vocation—self-identity, lifestyle and mission—are privileged contexts of both forms of personal encounter with the Lord. A man and a woman called to marriage meet God directly as individual persons. They encounter God also indirectly in each other, in their conjugal life, in their respective ministries and careers, in their children, in their families of origin and in other significant persons. A celibate encounters the Lord directly, as well as indirectly through solitude, personal consecration, community, ministry and significant people. A single man or woman encounters God directly and indirectly through his/her single mode of living, ministry and significant others.

E. Singlehood: Living a Certain Independence

Even a casual observer will note that most single people are independent individuals. Whether by choice or by circumstance, they make do for themselves. A more discerning observer will further note that independence is a key factor in a single person's encounter with God. A certain independence is an essential ingredient in the single mode of living and relating.

In marriage the Lord consecrates two persons in love. God thereby enables them to consecrate themselves to God and to each other in such a way that they share their lives together. They become one (Gen 2:24; Mark 10:8), yet without suffering loss to their individuality. That consecration renders them unmarriageable to anyone else for as long as they both live, and it establishes them in a particular vocational *interdependence.*

In celibacy, the Lord consecrates a man or a woman, enabling that person to consecrate him/herself to Christ for his sake and for the sake of the Gospel (Mark 10:29). That consecration renders the celibate unmarriageable to anyone at all (Matt 19:12) and establishes the celibate in a special *dependence* upon the person of Jesus.

God consecrates the single person to God in such a way that in response s/he chooses to be unmarried, yet remains marriageable. S/he chooses also not to be a personally consecrated celibate, yet is open to being drawn in that direction if God wills. The single person opts for a middle course which celebrates and witnesses a singular dimension of Christian *independence.*

The word "independence" as such does not occur in Scripture. However, the term "free" (*haphshí* in Hebrew, *eleútheros* in Greek) is commonplace: "Let the oppressed go free" (Isa 58:6); "If the Son makes you free, you shall be free indeed" (John 8:36). In virtually every instance where the Bible speaks of freedom, there is reference to either the political sphere (free from slavery and foreign domination) or the interior life (free from the servitude of sin, Rom 6:18; the domination of one's passions, Rom 7:23; the Law, Gal 4:21-31; death, Rom 6:21-23; etc.).

In laying down the characteristics of true discipleship (e.g., Matt. 5:3-12; John 13:34-35), Jesus never implies that a mature Christian can be only married or celibate. Admittedly, he does not specifically extol the single life, but neither does he exclude it. The following logion of the Lord applies equally to young and old, to Jew and gentile, to slave and free person, to married, celibate and single:

> If you make my word your home,
> you will be my disciples.
> You will learn the truth,
> and the truth will set you free (John 8:31-32).

Christian independence differs radically from stoic freedom. Stoicism postulates that the virtuous find happiness in themselves. Thus, they are independent of the external world which they have supposedly overcome by mastering self, passions and emotions.[2] The New Testament, however, views the Stoic response of self-mastery as inadequate because it is self-centered rather than Christ-centered.

Scripture posits that our freedom as children of God is not primarily the effect of control over the environment or the result of sheer self-determination. Our freedom flows from the transforming and purifying activity of God in us and around us. The crux of our weakness lies within us (Rom 7:16-20), and to address it requires much self-discipline. Yet, we cannot attain Christian dominion over ourselves purely by our own initiative (Rom 7:14-25, 8:18-25). The human condition is inherently deficient, and deficiency can yield only more deficiency. To have hold of ourselves is to grasp insufficient being. Self-preservation by stoic means would cause the destruction of our true self. Therefore, to find ourselves we must lose ourselves in Christ (Matt 10:39). To attain self-control, we must surrender control to the Lord. To be free from the slavery of sin, we must become servants of God (Rom 7:24-25).

How does Christian freedom, or independence, come about? It is by God's initiative:

> It is for freedom that Christ has set us free . . .
> You are called [by God] to be free . . . (Gal 5:1, 13).

How is that gift realized in us? It is: through our commitment of faith in the Lord Jesus (Rom 7:25); through our hope in life everlasting (Rom 6:22); through our love of Truth who is Christ (John 8:32; 14:6).

[2]See *TDNT*, II:487–502.

Evangelical freedom is for all God's children, regardless of lifestyle and ministry. It is the freedom to be totally dependent on Father, Son and Spirit. Thus, the independence characteristic of the single person remains within that all-embracing dependency. A single person is independent of another human being in contradistinction to the vocational interdependence of a husband and wife. A single person is free also from the mode of dependence between Christ and an individual which is specific to celibacy. Yet, a single person profoundly belongs to God and intimately interrelates with family members, friends and colleagues.

God wills single independence for certain persons. Moreover, that independence is a divinely chosen milieu in which the Lord transforms and purifies them.

F. Principles for Discerning a Positive Choice of the Single Life

People can be left single for innumerable reasons: "No one ever proposed to me"; "I could not make it in the religious life"; "I fear commitment"; etc. The following, however, are some of the more significant indications of a vocational choice to remain single.

1) *A Certain Inner Completeness*

For a single person, Christian independence flows from a basic self-reliance, coupled with a certain completeness without a conjugal relationship and without a celibate consecration. Since no man or woman is an island, a single individual maintains vital relationships with the Lord and with many people. Nevertheless, the single person does not need the special relatedness of marriage or of celibacy to attain the inner completeness of a mature adult and of a committed disciple.

What makes that inner completeness possible is not independence *per se,* but rather God's willing the single life for that individual. Singlehood is this person's vocational lifestyle. Jesus addresses these words as much to single people as to anyone else:

> You did not choose me.
> No, I chose you and commissioned you to go forth
> and to bear lasting fruit (John 15:16).

2) *The Practice of Single Chastity*

In the realm of psychosexual development, each Christian is called to practice chastity in a manner consonant with his/her maturity, lifestyle and mission. There is a Christian chastity characteristic of married couples, another specific to engaged couples and one particular to celibates. There is also a mode of chastity proper to single persons.

The example of dating illustrates something of the differences which exist among those various modes of chastity. By dating, we understand being open to letting a relationship move in the direction of courtship and possible marriage. Thus, an engaged or a married man would be unfaithful to his commitment if he dated other women. A husband could go out to dinner with a female friend, but it would have to be without availability for romance. A wife may take a long stroll with a priest. Yet, if they were dating one another, there would be a quality quite other than friendship in their encounter. Likewise a nun would be lacking fidelity if she dated. Single persons, however, are free to date other single people as much as they wish, provided they do not manipulate their dates or use them egotistically.

3) *A Sense of Purpose*

In order to make a vocational choice of the single life, a man or a woman needs a sense of purpose. S/he must have some awareness of being called by God to singlehood. The individual does not have to know precisely the Lord's will. Yet, a sense of meaningfulness prevails, even if vague and undefined. "I am serving God and others the way I am, and I am comfortable with that." "God seems to want me to become myself this way, and I am satisfied."

4) *Mature Involvement*

The quality of a person's involvement in society and in specific human relationships can indicate a positive choice of the single life. Isolation—as distinct from solitude—is always negative. In order that singlehood have a growth-producing influence on an individual's development, mature interaction with married, single and celibate persons of both sexes, as well as with society at large, is both normal and necessary.

CHAPTER 21

Modalities of the Single Life

Singlehood can have a variety of meanings. No specific concept, notion or definition embraces all facets of the single life. Marriage is highly institutionalized by both society and the Church. Celibacy is institutionalized to a large extent by the Church, but less so than marriage. Singlehood, on the other hand, is not institutionalized at all.

Singlehood can be lived in a great diversity of forms, ways and contexts. At least two of these forms are undesirable, even if they do occur with some frequency: 1) There are situations where in effect a single man and a single woman are "married" to each other. Legally, they are spouses. However, for all practical purposes they are two single people living under the same roof who may occasionally share the same bed. 2) There are professed "celibates" who are far from being personally consecrated. Even though they opt to remain unmarried, they are in their attitude and private life anything but unmarriageable for the sake of Christ and the Gospel.

An elaborate church wedding does not make a marriage, unless God has called the two partners together. Nor does ordination or a public vow ceremony make a celibate, unless the candidate has an authentic vocation coupled with a free response to it. People who have made vows of marriage or celibacy without being called by God are in reality single. Moreover, it would seem more constructive for them to admit that fact and to begin discerning their God-intended vocational lifestyle. Any way of life which is not an authentic vocation impedes continuing growth, whether emotional, psychological or spiritual. Whatever is true is ultimately best for all concerned.

In the previous chapter, we presented salient features of a vocation to singlehood and reasons for positively choosing that lifestyle: a professional career, dedication to a cause, preference for independence, etc. In this chapter, we take up certain modalities of the single life. These lifestyles are generally associated with singlehood, yet their vocational dimension is often overlooked. These modalities include: divorce, widowhood, homosexuality, single parenthood, infirmity, the situation of a person both unmarried and a former celibate.

A. Divorce

When the Lord calls two people together in matrimony, it is for life (Matt 19:1-9). A divorce in this case is but a legal instrument of separation. In actual fact, the two spouses remain married before God. From a vocational perspective, these divorced persons are unmarriageable to anyone else until the death of one of them. Yet, the couple no longer live together. Spiritually then, their lifestyle reflects some aspects of singlehood (by reason of their legal separation) as well as some aspects of married life (by reason of their lifelong covenant).

Unmarriageable divorced Christians encounter God in their awkward situation of living apart and yet being wedded.[1] Their individual lifestyles participate in both singlehood and married life, without being completely either.

Some divorced couples were never called by God to marry one another in the first place. If God has not united them, they are still marriageable from a vocational point of view. These divorced persons are in reality single. Therefore, all the principles of discernment related to the single life apply to them.

B. Widowhood

Widowhood contains at least four different modalities of being and relatedness:

1) Contrary to what some people assume, not all widows and widowers are interiorly single. Yes, their spouses have died and the juridical bonds of matrimony have terminated.

[1]See *Spiritual Journey,* 13–25.

But spiritually, many widows and widowers remain as covenanted to their spouses in death as in life, if not more so. Moreover, these persons remain as spiritually unmarriageable to anyone else as before their partners died.

We are not referring here to the widow or widower who is blocked at the denial phase of bereavement or who lives in a world of fantasy. Rather, we are speaking of transformed conjugal love in a deeply spiritual and mature person. With the death of the partner, the survivor's marriage enters an entirely new phase. Instead of the relationship ending with the passing of the spouse, it is transformed radically in the direction of spirit.

Toward the end of their earthly sojourn and after lengthy maturation, some married couples cross a threshold of union wherein they become as much in-love as is possible this side of the resurrection. They experience something of what complete union with each other in God will be. Married persons in-love may reach not only a degree of Spiritual Marriage with the Lord in their interior life,[2] but also a veritable "spiritual marriage" in their conjugal life.

The awareness of a mysterious need to die not only to self but to this mortal existence begins to impress itself upon them. This "death wish" is not a morbid presentiment, but the result of love yearning for consummate union beyond the limitations of earthly modes of relating. The lovers come to experience that only in passing beyond the constraints of this life can being-in-love reach its hoped for perfection. Thus, progress in loving opens lovers to desire passage through death so that they may be perfectly in-love with each other in God for all eternity. It is in this vein that the Beloved (the Bridegroom) in the Song of Songs attests:

> Love is as strong as death,
>   its ardor as unyielding as the grave.
> It burns like blazing fire,
>   like the very flame of Yahweh.
> Love no flood can quench,
>   no torrents drown (Cant 7:6-7).

[2]See ibid., 212–222.

Not even death can end the communion of two spouses in-love. On the contrary, death accelerates the spiritualization of their bond. The following sentiments express something of this mystery:

> I am in-love with you as much as I can be in this life.
> To love you more,
>   I must pass through death into eternity.
> I am in-love with you now and forever.

The survivor's existential inability to become otherwise remains in effect, but now in a transformed and transcendent manner. That threshold marks the apex of spiritual conjugal relationship in this life. Thus, the surviving partner yearns for the ultimate consummation of their marriage in eternity.

2) Some widows and widowers move inexorably in the direction of celibacy. Whether or not they make a formal consecration, the inner dynamics of their lifestyle bespeaks celibacy of heart for the sake of Christ and the gospel (Mark 10:29).

So profoundly spiritual is the relationship between some widows/widowers and Christ as well as between them and their departed spouses that modalities of both celibacy and spiritual marriage with the deceased coexist. In these cases, a person's inner thrust is beyond both marriage and celibacy as we ordinarily understand those terms. There is an experience of mystical espousal with Jesus and with the departed spouse at the same time. Perhaps that factor explains in part the special recognition of some widows in the early Church (see, for example, 1 Tim 5:3-16).

3) Many widows and widowers do remain single in the usual sense, either until remarriage or for the rest of their lives. These persons encounter God in a special way through their widowhood as well as in their families, particularly in their children and grandchildren.

4) Some situations are not widowhood in the strict sense because the two lovers were never formally married. Yet, the interior development of one of those persons unfolds in a way analogous to widowhood. Two examples come to mind: a) A man's fiancée dies before their marriage. Their love is such that it renders him incapable of ever marrying anyone else. b) A woman may be in love with a married man or with a celibate.

Yet, she does not want to break up the marriage or interfere with the celibate consecration. Her love is such that it makes her unable to marry anyone else.

We can envisage many possible emotional and psychological disturbances in connection with the above examples. Nonetheless, the situations in which those people find themselves can be integral to an authentic vocation to a modality of the single life.

C. Homosexuality

Sexual orientation can be imaged as a continuum with homosexuality and heterosexuality at opposite poles, and bisexuality situated midway between them. Along the continuum are varying intensities. Thus, a person may be more or less homosexual, bisexual, or heterosexual. Furthermore, the same person may move in one direction or the other as his/her sexual orientation evolves and according to a variety of life situations. For example: 1) Psychological professionals in general recognize that many males who are predominately heterosexual pass through a homosexual phase during their psychosexual development. 2) A basically heterosexual individual may be prompted to engage in homosexual practices during a period of incarceration when opposite-sex activity is not possible.

Homosexuality is a complex issue. What is it? What causes it? How might a person best deal with it? There is no consensus of opinion to those questions even among experts. Moreover, the emotional overtones which so frequently accompany discussions related to these intricate issues make impartial deliberation difficult.

As for ourselves, we accept homosexuality as part of the human condition. The homosexual orientation of many sincere Christians is an involuntary situation which they cannot change even with goodwill and professional help. They experience their homosexuality as an inclination which they must accept, integrate into their self-identity and let be a catalyst for their growth in holiness.

A person with a primarily homosexual orientation is not attracted romantically, sexually or genitally to anyone of the opposite sex. For that reason, s/he is not disposed to marriage in the traditional Judeo-Christian sense. Generally speaking, that individual is unmarriageable to a person of the opposite sex by reason of sexual orientation. Yet, that unmarriageability differs from the unmarriageability of a celibate at heart.

Many homosexual persons tend toward the single life by reason of their sexual orientation. They may be also called to the single life by God.

Rare though it is, the Lord does occasionally call a homosexually oriented individual to marriage with someone of the opposite sex. More frequent, however, are instances where closet gays or lesbians enter juridical marriages in order to mask their homosexuality.

God can call a homosexual person to celibacy too. When the Lord does so, the person is called to celibacy at heart. Some gays and lesbians, however, choose a lifestyle that appears celibate, but which lacks personal consecration. For them, celibacy by circumstance seems to be a more desirable option than remaining overtly single.

Everyone needs to love and to be loved. Everybody must have some intimacy with others. This is as true of homosexual persons as of bisexual or heterosexual individuals. It is as true also of celibates as of married people. There exists a responsible mode of chastity for engagement, one for marriage, another for celibacy, one for singlehood. The gospel invites all persons—whatever their sexual orientation—to implement their needs for human love and intimacy in accordance with their vocational way of life.

Single gays and lesbians encounter God not only in their single life, but also in their homosexual situation. Their sexual orientation is a major facet of their life and lifestyle. It is a key instrument and matrix of their transformation in God. They need neither fear their homosexuality nor be ashamed of it, since God deifies them not in spite of it but in and through it.

D. Single Parenthood

For better or for worse, like it or not, single parents—whether men or women—are definitely on the increase in our society. Some have been married and are now widowed, separated or divorced. Others have never wed, and may or may not eventually marry.

Once a mother or a father, always a mother or a father. Even in eternity, a unique relationship between procreator and offspring endures. However, the phrase "single parenthood" ordinarily refers to a temporary lifestyle. This way of life persists for as long as the child or adolescent needs direct parenting, and it usually ceases when the teenager or young adult leaves home to begin a life on his/her own.

The presence of a child or adolescent—together with primary responsibility for his/her nurturing and upbringing—enormously modifies the particulars of a single parent's lifestyle. When God calls a parent and an offspring together in this manner, their relationship and shared life become crucial to each other's spiritual development. Each encounters God in a unique way in the other, as well as in the life which they share together with all its advantages and disadvantages, joys and frustrations.

E. Infirmity

People with certain illnesses almost of necessity end up single. These infirmities can be emotional, psychological or physical. We all know examples of retarded or insane individuals. Persons who are paralyzed or who have cerebral palsy more often than not remain single. Regardless of the nature or the source of the illness, God encounters these men and women in the single life which is more or less forced upon them by their condition.

A few people with permanent infirmities do enter into successful marriages. Others live authentic celibate lives, whether privately or in association with a religious institute. Most, however, remain single. The latter need to eventually choose their singlehood as a way of life. For sure, they did not choose the circumstances. Yet, in order to grow interiorly they have to go forward positively with the lifestyle which their condition imposes.

Many of these single persons—whom people consider unfortunate—possess a vigorous spiritual life. They are veritable contemplatives.[3] They are often interiorly the most active contributors to a world that seems to have victimized them.

If God loves and looks after the poor in a very special manner, then the Lord must cherish preeminently the permanently infirm.

F. The Situation of Former Celibates Who Are Now Unmarried

The phrase sometimes used in the past to describe the effect of passing from celibacy to the single life was "reduced to the lay state." That phrase was misleading and theologically incorrect. Before God, no one was ever raised above others to the clerical or religious states in the first place. As far as vocational lifestyle is concerned, a former celibate would more accurately be said "to have resumed the single life."

Most people leave the celibate life in order to marry. This is especially true of persons who seek dispensation from religious vows or who resign from presbyterial ministry. Occasionally, however, we find individuals who at one time professed celibacy, yet presently experience their vocation in such a way that it includes neither formal celibate consecration nor matrimony. Basically their lifestyle is single, but frequently with a distinct vocational consciousness towards some apostolate. Many of these persons make excellent lay missionaries at home or abroad.

If former celibates do in fact have a vocation to celibacy—despite their dispensation or resignation—they will move inevitably in the direction of a private consecration. If they do not have a celibate calling, they will enter more deeply into the single life and become increasingly open to the possibility of marriage.

Many celibates by circumstance—whether diocesan priests or religious men and women—are, in terms of their inner attitude and their basic lifestyle, more in line with this modality

[3]See Pierre Teilhard de Chardin, "The Significance and Positive Value of Suffering," *Human Energy* (New York: Harcourt, 1969) 48–52; "The Spiritual Energy of Suffering," *Activation of Energy* (New York: Harcourt, 1970) 247–249; *O Blessed Night,* 168–170; *Receptivity,* 106–109.

of the single life than with celibacy for the sake of Christ and the gospel.

G. Concluding Remarks

The single life is for many people an authentic vocational lifestyle. As such, it witnesses in a special way to the freedom of the children of God. Signs authenticating a possible calling to singlehood include:

- experience of a certain inner completeness without either marriage or celibacy;
- ability to practice single chastity;
- sense of purpose in the single life;
- capacity for mature involvement with a variety of persons and activities.

For someone called by God to singlehood, this lifestyle constitutes a crucial vocational matrix in which the person matures emotionally, psychologically and spiritually. Some people experience their calling to singlehood eventually in terms of a vocational imperative. Many do not. Vocational imperatives are associated more with the lifelong consecration of marriage and celibacy. For an authentic sense of calling to singlehood a general awareness or a vague inclination suffices. A vocation to the single life does not of itself postulate permanent commitment. It is enough that the vocational dimension of singlehood focus on the present, the here and now, letting tomorrow take care of itself (Matt 6:33).

For some people the single life is a response in faith to God's initiative. It is not just something left over or for someone merely left out. The single life as a vocation is more than nonmarried or non-celibate. It is a positive and spiritually meaningful choice, even when certain human factors force these individuals to be single. From a relational perspective, singlehood as an Christian vocational lifestyle is a freely chosen expression of the person's relatedness to God, to self, to others and to creation.

CONCLUSION

Vocation and Faith, Hope and Love

Throughout this book we have painstakingly studied the key signs for discerning vocations to marriage, celibacy and singlehood. We highlighted the ontological, moral and spiritual imperatives toward lifelong commitment which God effects within persons called to marriage and celibacy. We stressed that threshold in evolving vocational consciousness wherein an individual experiences a calling to one of those basic lifestyles in terms of an existential inability to become otherwise. A vocation to singlehood does not necessarily engender a lifelong commitment. Concerning that calling, we identified some of its more common signs and modalities.

The specifically Christian feature of each vocational lifestyle is love. First, God's unique love for us sets our vocational direction in motion. Then, our evolving love for the Lord awakens our desire to live according to God's design. God's initiative and our desire for what the Lord wills flow from mutual encounter in love. Thus, at some point what God wills for us in terms of lifestyle and what we most deeply seek for ourselves converge. Ultimately, we yearn to choose freely the way in which the Lord calls us to live.

Most of us have to commit ourselves to considerable searching and listening before we intuit what we really desire and what God wants for us. We need to discern. Discernment is the faith process which enables us to ascertain what God is moving us to freely choose. In vocational discernment we try with the Spirit's guidance to plumb the depths of God in us, to discover which lifestyle accords with who we are becoming in Christ and to actualize that direction in our lives.

The crucial question is, therefore: How do we discern in love? The response can only be: By faith and in hope.

> [For] love believes all;
> love hopes all (1 Cor 13:7).

Faith and hope are like the eyes and the ears of love. They provide love with the means of seeing and listening.

Faith is light, vision, insight, while remaining dark, mysterious and Spirit-imbued. Faith enables us on an intuitive level to become conscious of our vocational thrust. Yet, faith also scrutinizes that awareness. It seeks some understanding of God's activity within us. It sifts out the various interior movements and cuts like a two-edged sword between the diverse spirits that play on our heartstrings. It unmasks illusions. It authenticates a genuine calling with both internal and external signs or principles of discernment.

The principles of discernment for callings to marriage, celibacy and singlehood are not computerized printouts of those vocations. They are not checklists on which we must score a certain percentile. They are rather faith-signs which affirm that we are approximating God's will as best we can discern. Those principles represent subtle observable indications of our loving communion with the Lord. Those indications then serve to encourage and in many instances impel us to move forward in our vocation.

Yes, faith enables us to see the signs of our calling. But that is not all. In faith, we commit ourselves to God through marriage or celibacy. In faith, we opt for God through singlehood. Even while enabling us to recognize the Lord's will in regard to our vocational direction, faith invites us to journey by night, to know by unknowing.

The experience of our vocation as an existential inability to be, become or do otherwise does not catapult us into a world of clarity, security and ease. On the contrary, our calling thrusts us into deeper mystery. Risk, struggle, tension and effort to discern continue to mark the journey forward.[1] Yet, that journey continues in the peace and joy of Christ. Our response to God's call remains a faith response. We commit ourselves

[1]See *Called by God,* 141–153.

daily to Father, Son and Spirit in faith amid all the changing circumstances of life:

> Each morning the Lord awakens me to listen,
> to listen like a disciple (Isa 50:4).

Because God's calling, our response and our vocational lifestyle evolve after we commit ourselves, hope also is essential in our vocational discernment and development. Hope pertains to what we have not yet attained. It is future-oriented. Hope is Christ in us straining forward toward the fullness of our transformation in him.

By hope, we depend on the indwelling Trinity to grace us with the wisdom, the perseverance and the courage to live out our calling. By hope, we rely on the Lord to accomplish God's purpose through our vocational lifestyle. We trust that our calling will be the milieu in which Christ brings us ever closer to consummate loving union in God. Hope affords us the confidence

> That the One who has begun this good work in [us]
> will carry it through to completion
> until the day of Christ Jesus (Phil 1:6).

APPENDIX

Priesthood: Ministry, Lifestyle or Both?

The term "priesthood" is used in connection with both the *priesthood of the faithful* and the *ordained priesthood*. These are also referred to respectively as the "universal priesthood" and the "ministerial priesthood" or the "presbyterate." The priesthood of the faithful is celebrated in the sacraments of baptism and confirmation.[1] It designates a person's incorporation into the general priestly mission of Jesus. The ordained priesthood, on the other hand, pertains to the sacrament of orders. Building upon the first, it incorporates a person into particular aspects of the priestly mission of Christ.

The question which we address here is this: In view of the theology of vocation from an evolutionary and relational perspective which we developed in our book *Called by God* and in view of the principles for discernment discussed throughout this present study, how do we reevaluate a calling to priesthood, whether of the faithful or of the ordained? In other words: Is it primarily a vocational lifestyle or a ministry, or both?

Since the presbyterate is one of the sacrament of orders, we consider also the other two orders: the diaconate and the episcopacy. Are they mainly vocational lifestyles or ministries, or both?

[1] "All the just belong to the priestly order" (St. Irenaeus of Lyons, *Against Heresies*, 4, 8, 3; *PG*, 7:995); "All [Christians] are priests because they are members of one and the same priesthood" (St. Augustine, *The City of God*, 20, 10; *PL* 41:676; *CCSL*, 48:720).

A. The Diaconate

In its most general sense *diákonos* in New Testament Greek refers to a servant; for example: a waiter at a meal (John 2:5), a steward of a master (Matt 22:13). Thus, Paul writes of Epaphrás as "a faithful *diákonos* of Christ" (Col 1:7), of Túchicus as a "servant in the Lord" (Col 4:7) and of himself as a servant of the Church (Col 1:24-25).

Nonetheless, an important distinction exists between those general usages and the specific application of the word to an ecclesial office. The introduction of the Letter to the Philippians suggests "deacon" in the latter sense:

> To all the saints in Christ Jesus at Philippi
> together with their bishops and deacons (1:1).

The First Letter to Timothy infers that the offices of bishop and deacon stand in close relationship. There the qualities of the one follow immediately the requirements for the other:

> A bishop must be above reproach,
> the husband of one wife,
> temperate, sensible, orderly, hospitable, able to teach . . .
> managing well his own family. . . .
> Deacons also are to be respectable persons . . .
> holding on to the mystery of faith . . .
> husbands of one wife and
> capable of managing well their households (3:2-12).

The history of the diaconate shows how diverse has been the understanding of this office over the centuries. Nonetheless, in the apostolic Church a deacon's function was essentially that of service: service to a bishop, service to the faithful, service at the Eucharist. The existence of deaconesses in the early Christian community is incontestable. Whether the references in Romans 16:1 and 1 Timothy 3:11, however, are to women offering their services to the community or to deaconesses in the sense of office-holders within the Church remains disputed.[2]

In terms of vocational discernment, therefore, we consider the diaconate more a ministry than a lifestyle. It accentuates

[2]See *TDNT*, II:88–93.

what the Lord calls a person *to do* for God and for God's people rather than *how* the Lord calls a person *to become* transformed. Thus, a deacon's ministry would be an ecclesial service, while his/her vocational lifestyle could be married, celibate or single.

B. The Presbyterate

In the New Testament, two Greek words are translated "priest": *hiereús* and *presbúteros.* Each is part of a broader word family, and each has an intricate history going back centuries into Hebrew thought and practice. Moreover, a variety of usages of those terms exist even in apostolic times.[3] Related to the first word family are expressions like hierarchy, reverence, sacred, temple, priesthood, priestly office, priestly ministry. From the second word family come such terms as presbyter, presbyterial college, presbytery.

Without too much oversimplification, *hiereús* means "priest" with emphasis on cultic sacredness and proclamation. It accentuates the aspect of being set apart for cultic ministry, temple sacrifice and preaching of God's word. The pristine meaning of *hierós* is holy, hallowed, divine.

Presbúteros, on the other hand, denotes "elder" in the sense of an ordained official leading a congregation. It refers to one who is responsible for the administration of both the spiritual and the material aspects of a local church. The pristine meaning of *présbus* is old man, senior ambassador, elder statesman.

Jesus does not use either word for priest in direct reference to himself or to his disciples. This may be due to the sometimes pejorative connotations associated with the terms (see Luke 10:30-37). Jesus did, however, exercise in a transcendent manner the sacrificial and mediative dimensions of the Hebraic priesthood. So true is this that the Letter to the Hebrews calls him "high priest" (*archiereús*) and develops a Christology and a theology of priesthood around that theme. Yet, nowhere does the New Testament speak of Jesus as *presbúteros*.

The First Letter of Peter underscores a universal priesthood:

> You [all believers in the Lord] are like living stones
> being built into a spiritual house.

[3]See *TDNT,* III:221-283; *TDNT,* VI:651-680.

You form a holy priesthood [*hieráteuma hágion*]
so as to offer spiritual sacrifices
acceptable to God through Jesus Christ (1 Pet 2:5).

That priesthood of the faithful is distinctly Christian since it includes the Gentiles and incorporates a Trinitarian insistence. Yet, the basic revelation that God's people are somehow priests goes back to the Sinai covenant:

Of all the peoples of the earth
you are my treasured possession.
Although the whole earth is mine,
you are to me a kingdom of priests [*mamlechém cohaním*],
a holy nation (Exod 19:5-6).

Acts 16:4 speaks of "the apostles and the presbyters" as a deliberative body in the context of a normative teaching office for the universal Church. The reference in James 5:14 regarding the anointing of the sick is to a ministerial presbyterate: "Let them summon the elders of the assembly."

Paul instructs Titus to "appoint presbyters in every city" (Titus 1:5) and then adds:

An elder should be without reproach,
a husband of one wife,
whose children are believers and not open to accusations
of being wild and unruly (Titus 1:6).

The next verse speaks of "the bishop" in the community and enumerates similar requirements. That Paul refers to elders in the plural and to bishop in the singular in successive verses implies that although their qualifications are similar, their ministries differ. That reference may suggest also that the episcopacy is in a ministerial sense the fullness of the presbyterate.

In terms of vocational self-identity, lifestyle and mission, the presbyterate is primarily a ministry, an office within the Church. In view of the distinctions we have been developing, the presbyterate is more accurately *what* the Lord calls a person *to do* for God and God's people then *how* the Lord calls a person *to become* transformed in God. Except for current ecclesial legislation, therefore, a Roman Catholic presbyter's vocational lifestyle could be married, celibate or single.

C. The Episcopacy

In the New Testament, the noun *epískopos* is used once of Christ (1 Pet 2:25) and four times of ecclesial office holders (Acts 20:28; Phil 1:1; 1 Tim 3:2; Titus 1:7). The Greek verb from which this noun is derived means to oversee in the sense of caring for, watching over, shepherding. Its meaning is rooted in the Hebrew Scriptures. For example, the Book of Numbers advises:

> Let Yahweh . . . appoint someone to guide the community . . . so that it is not like sheep without a shepherd (27:16-17).

1 Peter 2:25 speaks of Jesus as "the Shepherd and Overseer of [our] souls." As such, Jesus possesses full knowledge of our inner development. He has completely sacrificed himself for us and mediates to us all that is divine.

The New Testament is not specific as to what constitutes the office of bishop. However, it does present bishops as overseers of congregational life in stable local communities which observe some ecclesial regularity. Their situation is in contrast to that of the itinerant charismatic preachers of the gospel like the apostles, prophets and certain teachers.[4] Even if the duties of bishops are not spelled out, their qualifications are: 1) moral reliability, 2) if married, that it be monogamous, 3) proof from their family life of ability to direct the community, 4) skill as teachers and preachers of the Word, 5) personal spiritual maturity and the wisdom that accompanies advanced age, 6) an integrity respected by Christians and non-Christians alike (1 Tim 3:1-7; Titus 1:5-9).

The New Testament does not speak of bishops, priests and deacons in a tripartite descending order, but the Apostolic Fathers do.[5] From the first century, therefore, the sacrament of orders comprises three distinct ministries: diaconate, presbyterate and episcopacy. These are also distinct vocations, although one can evolve into another. They are vocations in terms of *what* God calls a person *to do* as an office holder and minister within the institutional Church.

[4]See *TDNT*, II:608–623.

[5]See for example St. Ignatius of Antioch (+ c. 107), *Letter to the Smyrnaeans*, 8 (*PG*, 5:707–718).

D. Priestly Ministry

We might say that the Christian theology and praxis of the priesthood has a four-thousand year history. In a sense, it begins with Abraham's encounter with Melchizedek (Gen 14:17-24). Its subsequent evolution throughout the Hebrew Scriptures and Jewish theocracy, culminating at the Last Supper, is multifaceted. From the Last Supper through the apostolic and patristic periods to the present, many different forms and expressions of priestly ministry have arisen.

Within that history, what constitutes the core of priestly ministry specifically as presbyter? (and *mutátis mutándis* also as bishop?) The fundamental characteristics are these:[6]

- to proclaim the Gospel by word and example;
- to celebrate the Eucharist, to preside over other liturgical functions and to administer the sacraments;
- to build up and to serve the local ecclesial community which in turn serves the world.

Since by reason of its Christic institution the Church is incarnate in society, those elements imply inculturation of the faith and stewardship of the Church's material goods.

E. Priestly Life

The priesthood is indeed a ministry. It is a service which God calls certain persons to exercise for the spiritual enhancement of the community. As such, the presbyterial vocation pertains to the *charísmata*—gifts bestowed by God within the Church especially for other's benefit. Yet, can the presbyterial vocation be also a mode of life, a vocational lifestyle? That is, can it pertain to *how* the Lord calls someone to become transformed in God? Yes, but in a way other than what many people envisage.

The key to the essence of priestly life is the person of Jesus specifically as *archiereús:* high priest. The Letter to the Hebrews

[6]See the documents of Vatican II related to the subject; *The Ministerial Priesthood* by the third Synod of Bishops in 1971; Paul VI and John Paul II on the topic; the documents prepared by the U.S.A.'s Bishops' Committee on Priestly Life and Ministry.

presents a compelling theology of this mystery.[7] We summarize only those elements which bear directly on our subject.

1) *Christ, the Sinless High Priest*

Jesus is priest because he is Son incarnate. As priest, he has a mission: universal salvation, redemption, liberation, transformation. Yet, his priestliness is more than something he is sent to accomplish. It is especially a way of being, an all-embracing, all-penetrating lifestyle. Jesus's priestly mission flows out of his priestly life. The Letter to the Hebrews proclaims many aspects of Christ as priest; for example:

- He is faithful (3:2-6).
- He is like us in all things, but without sin (4:14-16).
- He is compassionate (5:1-7).
- He has learned to obey through suffering (5:8-10).
- He has established a radically new way of being priest (7:1-28).

The same epistle elaborates two other aspects of the priesthood of Jesus which we wish to develop in the context of Christian participation in his priestly life. They are:

- Christ-priest-mediator and
- Christ-priest-victim in his own sacrifice (Heb 8-10).

a) *Christ-Priest-Mediator.* Jesus as priest is mediator in virtue of his incarnation. When the Word became flesh and pitched his tent in our midst (John 1:14), all that is uncreated yet creating met all that is created and becoming. Divinity was made mortal; eternity was made temporal.

Yet, if Christ is mediator in virtue of his incarnation, he is even more so by reason of his resurrection. For God not only met humanity but also communed and interacted with it in such a way as to transform it, to deify it, to divinize it. From the moment that the hypostatic union occurred in the womb of Mary, Jesus was truly divine and truly human. But like us, his humanity did not reach the fullness of its development until his personal death/resurrection. Christ rose all God. That is,

[7]See *TDNT*, III:274–283.

in and through his paschal mystery, Jesus's humanity became totally transformed by his divinity. In his person, the human and the divine met and communed in such a way that his humanity became completely divinized.

For Jesus, mediation is a dimension of theandric being which brings forth a transcendent effect. The New Testament captures something of that mystery in the phrase "once and for all":

> Christ has been made manifest once and for all
> to abolish sin by the sacrifice of himself (Heb 9:26).
>
> Christ died for sins once and for all . . .
> to bring you to God (1 Pet 3:18).

Western modes of conceptualization tend to perceive mediation mainly as an activity which someone performs; for example, mediating a labor dispute. Yet, in relation to Christ and our participation in the mediative aspect of his priesthood, mediation is more fundamentally a way of being and becoming. It thus pertains to self-identity and vocational lifestyle.

b) *Christ-Priest-Victim in His Own Sacrifice.* As priest, Jesus himself is the oblation. Being mediator and being self-oblation the priestly Jesus is described as *a way*—a radically "new and living way" (Heb 10:20)—back to the Father (Heb 7:19). The culminating point on this return journey is his sacrifice of himself in his death/resurrection. The priesthood of Jesus did not put him in the spotlight of human attention. Instead, it thrust him into lowliness and solidarity with fellow pilgrims (Heb 2:17; 4:15). This aspect of the Savior's life caused offense to many (1 Cor 1:23-25).

Unlike the Levites and the Cohens before him, Christ's sacrifice was not by substitutionary expiation, but by total personal self-giving (Heb 9:28, 7:27). Jesus as priest was victim in his own sacrifice. The blood which he offered was not that of goats or heifers, but his very own. He did not offer some-*thing;* he offered himself. Jesus brought to his self-oblation every facet of his life. Therefore, rather than purely cultic and physical immolation, Christ as priest emphasizes the continuous fulfillment of the Father's will in a lifestyle permeated with radical obedience and love (Heb 10:5-9). The salvific act whereby Jesus redeemed us was not precisely his expiration on the cross. *The act* of salvation was rather the culmination in Christ's death and resurrection of a lifelong obedience to the Father and love for God and humankind. Thus, his physical expiration was a symbol or sacrament of his theandric obedience and love.

Also unlike the Levitical sacrifices which were performed once a year or once in a while, the immolation of Jesus was once-and-for-all (Heb 7:27, 9:24-28). The divinity of the person offering his human life in sacrifice makes his self-oblation an act which transcends time and space. Moreover, in virtue of Christ's descent and resurrection his self-oblation becomes immanent in all creation.

2) *Sinners Called to Participate in Christ's Sinless Priesthood*

If, instead of describing the Levitical priesthood, Hebrews 5:1-3 were to epitomize priestly life in light of the priesthood of Jesus, the text might read thus:

> Every person called by God to the priestly life
> in imitation of Christ
> is chosen from among men and women
> to mediate between God and God's people
> and to offer him/herself to the Lord in self-oblation.
> This priestly person deals gently
> with the ignorant and the erring
> because s/he also is beset by weakness.
> For that reason, this person must offer continuous
> self-oblation for him/herself and for others.

Being mediator and being victim in one's own sacrifice thus constitute the quintessence of priestly life.

a) *Participating in Christ's Mediation.* How are we mediators in imitation of and in participation with the priestly mediation of Jesus?

Ordinarily, we consider mediation an activity, and a rather exacting one at that. To mediate is to reconcile differences between parties, to bring about an accord, to act as intermediary in effecting or communicating something. In the context of priesthood, this activity could entail proclaiming the word of God, administering the sacraments, listening to and guiding people on their spiritual journey.

But even more than something we do, mediation in the context of priesthood expresses something essential about how we are. It designates a mode of being, an inner quality, an all-penetrating attitude of remaining lovingly and consciously receptive to the activity of God in and through oneself in relation to others. *Being mediator*—in contradistinction to *doing mediation*—entails letting the Lord save, redeem, liberate, transform someone through oneself.

Doing mediation can be a specific mission to which God calls some people. Ministering as presbyter necessarily implies doing mediation. Participation in the priesthood of the faithful can include a vocation to do mediation, but not necessarily so.

However, being mediator—not just in a sense applying to all the baptized and confirmed, but as a specific Christian vocational lifestyle—is a different issue. Although all God's people are called to an inner disposition which allows the Lord to mediate through them to others, God calls certain persons to make self-oblation the core of their life. The Lord moves them to accentuate consciously, willingly, and radically the priestly dimension of their baptismal and confirmational commitment. Being mediator becomes a veritable lifestyle for them. The accent does not fall so much on *what* they do as mediators, since they may "do" virtually nothing in the conventional sense. Rather, the accent falls upon *how* they become themselves for God and for others.

Thus, God can call to the priestly life, for example, a married woman dying of AIDS. Moreover, the Lord need not call every ordained presbyter to priestly mediation as an all-embracing lifestyle.

b) *Participating in Christ's Self-Oblation.* Being victim with Christ in his sacrifice is a unique vocation and a unique lifestyle. The self-offering characteristic of a priestly way of life is unconditional, all-embracing and unto death. In order to be a vocational lifestyle, however, that self-sacrifice has to be a response to a special calling by God.

By "sacrifice" we understand doing or refraining from doing something which apart from love, a sense of calling and obedience one would never do or abstain from. By "victim" we mean that the one performing the oblation is at the same time agent, subject and object of the act. Thus, *I* offer *myself* to God *for myself* and for others. I am a victim of love—love of the Lord and of others. By "vocation," we infer that although in a general way all God's people are called to self-sacrifice the Lord calls certain persons to make self-oblation the core of their life. God moves them to accentuate in a radical way this priestly dimension of their baptismal and confirmational commitment. Self-oblation becomes for them a veritable lifestyle. The accent does not fall so much on *what* they do as victims. Rather, it falls upon *how* they become themselves for God and for others.

The response to a vocation to immolate oneself is radical obedience and love. The person called to the priestly life—to a lifestyle of mediation and self-oblation unto death—is invited to a particular expression of obedience to the Father's will (Luke 22:42) and to a unique form of consecration in love (John 13:1; 17:18, 22-23). Forgiveness and reconciliation occur only when an intensity of obedience and love outweighs the disobedience and selfishness which caused a hurt (i.e., evil, pain, sin).

Therefore, the priestly life as an all-embracing lifestyle of being mediator and being self-oblation is a special imitation of the priesthood of Christ. Everyone living this priestly life is not victim of love in the same way. Each vocation is unique to the person called. In some instances the vocation is so spiritual that no one other than the victim and a spiritual director is aware of its existence. In other situations, God alone knows.

St. Thérèse of the Child Jesus is an example of one who lived the priestly life both as mediator and as self-oblation. On the Feast of the Holy Trinity, 1895, she composed the following prayer to express her consciousness and willingness to embrace fully this lifestyle:

> In order to live in a single act of perfect love, I OFFER MYSELF AS A VICTIM OF HOLOCAUST TO YOUR MERCIFUL LOVE. I ask you to consume me incessantly, allowing the waves of *infinite tenderness* contained within you to overflow into my soul. May I thus become a *martyr* of your *Love,* my God!
>
> May this martyrdom, after having prepared me to appear before you, finally cause me to die and may my soul fly directly into the eternal embrace of *your Merciful Love.*
>
> I want, my *Beloved,* at each beat of my heart to renew this offering to you an infinite number of times, until the shadows

having disappeared I can tell you of my *Love* in an *Eternal Face-to-Face!*[8]

While that prayer focuses principally on self-oblation, the element of mediation is implicit. That element was made explicit, however, in Pius XI's proclamation of St. Thérèse as patroness of missions in 1927.

God does not seem to call every deacon, presbyter, bishop and pope to the priestly life in the sense that we have described. Many priests and bishops do not live this quality of priestly life and do not experience—at least at this point in their earthly sojourn—a calling to do so.

Yet, when the person with a vocation to priestly life is also an ordained presbyter, the congruity of presbyterial ministry and of priestly lifestyle blend into one singularly expressive mode of being, becoming and ministering. St. John Vianney, the Curé of Ars, is a striking example. There are many others.

F. Concluding Observations

Several conclusions flow from the above reflections:

1) A person called by God to the *priestly life* can be either a man or a woman; married, single or celibate. Furthermore, s/he can be wholeheartedly engaged in the apostolic, the contemplative or the eremitical life (or some other Christian lifestyle) at the same time as living out a calling to the priestly life. Priestly life is a vocation within a vocation.

2) Regarding *ordained presbyterial ministry,* there are sound theological grounds for these pastoral options:

a) The ministry could be full-time or part-time. Like baptism and confirmation, ordination imparts a permanent charism to the person receiving it. However, a calling to presbyterial ministry need not automatically imply that the person must make a full-time commitment to that specific service. Practice of part-time

[8]See *Story of a Soul,* trans. John Clarke (Washington: ICS Publications, 1976) 277.

presbyterial ministry can be traced back to the beginning of Church history.

b) The person called to presbyterial ministry could be a man or a woman; married, single or celibate. It would greatly enhance the quality of the presbyterate as well as the life of the Church if there were married, single and celibate clergy of both sexes. Not only would this situation be better in many respects, but also it seems truer to God's way of imparting vocations.

3) Since deacons require maturity and experience, it would be precipitous to ordain them before early adulthood is well established (i.e., mid-twenties or early thirties). If a presbyter is truly an "elder," a candidate would ordinarily have attained midlife before ordination (i.e., late thirties or early forties). Bishops must be the most mature and experienced of all. Therefore, latelife seems appropriate for their ordination (i.e., fifties or sixties).

Sic fínis líbri, non aútem quaeréndi.